Advancing Native Missions

Voices

In The Wilderness

*100 Inspirational Snippets of
Courage and Faith From Around the World*

Edited By Douglas C. Hsu

ANM
publishers

Scripture quotations are taken from the HOLY
BIBLE, NEW INTERNATIONAL VERSION.
Copyright 1973, 1978, 1984 by the International
Bible Society. Used by permission of Zondervan
Bible Publishers.

ISBN: 0-97153460-8

Published by Advancing Native Missions
P.O. Box 5303
Charlottesville, VA 22905

Layout by Megan Johnson
Johnson2Design
www.Johnson2Design.com
Rustburg, VA

Printed in the United States of America

To the native missionaries around the world
whose voices continue to cry out in the wilderness

Contents

Contents

Acknowledgements

As with many books, this one has taken the staff of Advancing Native Missions many years to write. In 1988 Carl Gordon and Benjamin "Bo" Barredo first dreamed of compiling testimonies from our native missionary brethren around the world into a devotional guide. Nearly ten years later, Wayne Wozniak began working full-time culling these testimonies from in-house files and personal interviews, while Jay Temple and Douglas Hsu started collecting testimonies from their field visits. Virginia Tobias and Robert Hewitt provided initial editorial assistance, and finally Douglas re-worked, edited, and assembled the complete manuscript for our first printing in 2001. Six years later, Douglas re-typed the entire manuscript from scratch and then extensively re-edited each story for this revised edition.

We owe a special thanks to all our overseas brethren who cooperated with us in this project by sitting for interviews and sending us reports by fax and email. This book could not have been written if they had not so openly shared their hearts with us. Thanks also goes to Michael Erkel for the cover design, to Bill James for his generous help in laying out and printing this book, and to our friends Gary and Linda who contributed towards the initial printing costs.

Finally, we acknowledge that our Lord Jesus Christ is the ultimate inspiration for, motivation behind, and enabler of this book. He is the One whom these "voices in the wilderness" proclaim, and He is the One who has given us the high privilege of sharing their voices in this volume.

Introduction

They all have three things in common—Rockeybell Adatura, Narayan Paul, and David Yone Mo, whose testimonies all appear in this volume.

First, they were all born and brought up in lands closed to foreign missionaries.

Second, they all came out of non-Christian backgrounds—Muslim, Hindu, and Buddhist—to become followers of Jesus Christ.

And third, they have all dedicated their lives to proclaiming the gospel among their own countrymen. We call them *native missionaries*, as opposed to foreign missionaries, because they are reaching their own people with the gospel.

Native missionaries are nothing new in the history of world evangelization. A man suffering from leprosy was healed by Jesus and immediately went out locally telling others what the Lord had done for him (Mark 1). A promiscuous woman from Samaria met the Lord and then led many in her village to follow Christ (John 4). A man from the region of the Gerasenes was delivered from demon possession and soon became a powerful evangelist in his area (Mark 5).

From the very beginning of the Christian era, native missionaries have been the primary means of bringing the gospel to the masses. They do not struggle with huge language, cultural, or geographical barriers. The Lord used them to reach lost people in the past, and He continues to use them today.

But most of us know very little about them, for various reasons. Many native missionaries lack fluency in English, do not have large prayer letter distribution networks, and lack access to email facilities.

Most live in regions of the world far from the gaze of the Western Christian media. Others could care less about publicizing themselves or their ministries.

However, we strongly believe that their voices *need to be heard* by those of us living in developed nations. We need their voices to *teach us* fundamental truths of practical Christianity that have been lost in our materialistic, feel-good, entertainment-driven culture. We need their voices *to inspire and challenge us* to adopt a higher standard of Christian living. And we need their voices *to spur us to pray*—for the lost, for our suffering brethren, and for ourselves. Hence the reason for this book.

The stories in this volume are true testimonies collected from our native missionary friends around the world. (In a few cases, names have been changed to protect the lives of those living in sensitive areas.) Advancing Native Missions (ANM) partners with native missionaries to help bring the gospel to the unreached in their corner of the world, through financial, prayer, material, and spiritual support. After reading these testimonies, if you wish to learn more about how you can be personally involved in supporting native missionaries, we invite you to consult the ANM information section at the end of this book.

It is our prayer that as you read and listen to these different voices, your heart would be stirred to pray, your spirit would be challenged to grow Christ-ward, and your soul would be moved to glorify God.

Douglas Hsu, Editor
Siliguri, West Bengal, India
March 2001

1
A Teacher's Dilemma

CUBA

"Is it true what I have heard, Mrs. Lopez? Are you a Christian?" The school principal's words slammed into Maria's heart.

"Yes, I am."

"Well, I don't know how you slipped through the cracks, but there can be no Christian teachers in this school," the principal firmly replied. "You have three days to give up your faith. If not, I will have to release you."

"With all due respect, Señora, I do not need three days to think about it," answered Maria. "I will never give up my faith."

"Well, you *should* think about it. If I fire you, your record will be permanently marked, and you will never work as a teacher again—at least not in this country!"

Maria spent the next three days in prayer. She loved her job. Not only did it provide an income for her family, but it also gave her an opportunity to shine like a star in the darkness. While the Cuban schools indoctrinated children with atheism, Maria strove to bring Christ's love into her classroom whenever possible. Day after day she had put her job in jeopardy.

Three days later, the principal met her in the hallway. "Have you made a decision?"

Her voice quavering slightly, Maria replied, "My decision was made many years ago. I will never give up my faith in Christ."

"Then you may come and sign your release form in the office."

Maria's heart pounded. How would she possibly provide for her family now?

"Lord," she prayed, "give me strength to go through this valley."

Maria packed up her belongings and made her way to the office. As she approached the door, she heard the sound of someone crying. She knocked, then entered. To her surprise, she found the principal weeping.

"What's the matter, Mrs. Gonzales?"

"I am so moved by your faith," she said, struggling to regain her composure. "Once I was a teacher, and a Christian also. When my director ordered me to give up my faith or give up my job, I chose to give up my faith. How I wish I had faith like yours to stand up for what I believed!"

Maria's eyes welled with tears as she prayed with her principal, leading her back into Jesus' waiting arms. Mrs. Gonzales assured her that as long as she was in charge of the school, Maria's job would be secure.

CR CR

"Let us hold unswervingly to the hope we profess, for he who promised is faithful."
HEBREWS 10:23

Lord, if I carefully reflect on the course of my life, I see that You have always been faithful to me. May I always be faithful to you!

2

A Strange Request

O ne day a thick overseas packet arrived in the mailbox of an American office. Inside were numerous pages containing thousands of Asian names, along with a strange request noted on top: "Please include these names in the Lamb's Book of Life." What prompted such an odd request?

Scattered throughout Southeast Asia in China, Vietnam, Laos, and Thailand are half a million people belonging to the White Miao tribe. For centuries they had practiced the only religion they knew: animism, the worship of evil spirits.

In 1993 a White Miao family was fiddling with their short-wave radio dial when they suddenly heard a man speaking in their own dialect. They were amazed: never before had they heard a radio broadcast in their own language. The news quickly spread like wildfire from home to home and village to village, "The radio is speaking our language! The radio is speaking our language!"

Throughout the White Miao villages, young and old alike began huddling around their short-wave radio sets every day to hear the broadcasts. The radio preacher spoke of a Great Spirit named Jesus who had come to set the White Miao free from having to serve evil spirits. He explained how Jesus was offering them a new life filled with peace and joy.

No one in the region had ever heard of this Great Spirit, so they all listened carefully to every word. The radio preacher exhorted them to forsake their idolatry and turn to Jesus. In time, the village leaders and family heads met together to discuss what they should do. After discussing among themselves, they decided that they would become Christians—all of them!

Without Bibles, missionaries, or any outside help except the radio messages, the White Miao began submitting every aspect of their lives to Jesus Christ. Whatever the radio pastor told them, they carefully obeyed. They heard that they should destroy their old gods, so they smashed their idols. After hearing about baptism, they dug large pits, filled them with water, and baptized each other. Today the number of White Miao believers has grown to at least 10,000 in China and 50,000 in Vietnam.

One day the radio pastor preached on the Lamb's Book of Life. "All who trust in Jesus have their names written on its pages, and only those whose names are written there shall enter the kingdom of heaven," he said.

The White Miao believers wanted to make sure that none of them would be left out of this book, so they sent a large packet with all their names to the American radio station broadcasting the messages!

కు

"Nothing impure will ever enter [heaven], nor will anyone who does what is shameful or deceitful, but only those whose names are written in the Lamb's book of life."

REVELATION 21:27

Lord, thank you for promising to write my name in the Lamb's Book of Life after I repented and received Jesus as my Savior. O might the names of all my friends and family members also be found there!

3
The Canceled Funeral

MYANMAR (BURMA)

D avid had already made up his mind to be the gang leader, and nobody could stand in his way. He whipped out a razor blade, snapped it in half, and stared his challenger in the face: "Let's get into a barrel and fight to the death with these!"

Fearful of the outcome, the other contender backed down, and David Yone Mo became the new leader of the Road Devils—the most notorious street gang in Myanmar. Under his leadership the Road Devils not only conquered the streets but also started engaging in large-scale drug trafficking, dealing in the world's highest-grade heroin. Business boomed, and before long David himself had become an addict.

Long ago David had turned his back on religion, refusing to side with either his Christian mother or his Buddhist father. Even after his marriage to Kathy, which started to fall apart because of his gang involvement and drug use, he kept refusing to give a second thought to God. In time, David's mother led Kathy to the Lord. Often David would return home drunk or high, only to find Kathy and his mother kneeling in prayer for his soul.

After several years of heroin use, David contracted viral hepatitis from dirty needles and was hospitalized. The doctor told his mother that he had less than a week to live. With tears in her eyes, she tucked a New Testament under his pillow and went home to make arrangements for her son's funeral.

Frightened and without hope in the final moments of his life, David reached under his pillow for the little book his mother had left behind. With no prior knowledge of the Bible, he opened it to Luke 23, the story of Jesus hanging on the cross between the two thieves. His heart was deeply touched by Jesus' reply to the repentant thief: *"Today you will be with me in paradise."* Realizing that it was still not too late for him to repent, he also asked Jesus to forgive him and save him.

Immediately David felt the Lord's power surge through his body. At that instant, he knew that the Lord had healed him and saved him! To the utter disbelief of the hospital staff, he was examined and found to be completely normal. Within a few days he was discharged, and his mother joyfully canceled his funeral!

Arriving home, David excitedly told his gang members what Jesus Christ had done for him. They made fun of him, predicting that his new religious "high" would not last long. But ignoring their remarks, he kept on telling them about the Lord. Within a few weeks, both of his top assistants had decided to accept the Lord.

David and his new converts dissolved the Road Devils and in its place founded a new Christian "gang"—the Myanmar Young Crusaders, a ministry to drug addicts and street gangs. Since then, thousands in Myanmar ranging from drug addicts to opium growers have come to know the Lord through this nationally-known ministry.

David's testimony reminds us that we should never give up praying for others, because the Lord's grace can bring even the toughest sinner to repentance.

"Therefore he is able to save completely those who come to God through him, because he always lives to intercede for them."

HEBREWS 7:25

Lord, let me always be faithful in praying for the salvation of the lost.

DAVID YONE MO, FOUNDER-DIRECTOR OF
MYANMAR YOUNG CRUSADERS, MYANMAR

4
The Wonder-Working God

W *hat if I pray for her and nothing happens?*

Pastor Meng was sitting at home one day when his heart was suddenly burdened for a particular village. Though he tried to brush it aside, the sense of urgency to visit this place kept on growing. Deciding at last that it must be the prompting of the Holy Sprit, he rounded up five other church members and set off along the mud-slicked roads through the pouring rain to reach the village.

When they arrived there, they saw a witch doctor dancing around the village chief's wife, who was very ill. Meng and his companions watched with a mixture of bewilderment and horror as the witch doctor performed different pagan rituals and called upon the various tribal gods to heal her. Meanwhile, the chief's wife continued to lie there, groaning in pain.

At first Meng and his companions did not know what to do. They knew it would not be wise to interrupt the all-night voodoo ceremony. Therefore, they decided just to remain in the background and pray continuously.

Early in the morning, one of the villagers noticed the six praying Christians and walked over to them. "The wife of our village chief is very ill," he explained. "We've tried everything, but our gods are not helping. Can you do anything for her?"

Meng was led into a small hut, where he saw the woman lying in great pain. Fear struck his heart. *What if I pray for her and nothing happens? What then will the chief and the rest of the villagers think?*

Meng started to pray, asking the Lord to display His glory and His might to the villagers by healing the woman. He found himself praying aloud in an unknown language. Although he could not understand what he was saying, he still felt led to continue praying in this way.

After he had finished, the woman stopped shaking and became calm. Within one hour she was back on her feet and ready to cook. Meanwhile, the amazed chief asked Meng, "How did you learn our language? Can you tell us more about your God?"

Meng was astonished. He realized that the Lord had miraculously equipped him to pray aloud in the villagers' own language. As a result, they were very eager to hear about the God who had just worked a wonder in their midst. Meng shared the gospel with them, and before long the entire village had accepted the Lord!

Is it not encouraging to know that the Almighty God still works wonders in our day?

☙❧

"And these signs will accompany those who believe: In my name they will drive out demons; they will speak in new tongues; ...they will place their hands on sick people, and they will get well."

MARK 16:17-18

Lord, I praise You for continuing to be the wonder-working God, displaying Your might so that all may believe in You!

5
Crumbling Doubts

Their only object under investigation: the Bible. Their mission: to prove Christianity wrong. Would they succeed?

Mohammed, Noor, and Abdul were three of the top Islamic scholars in Indonesia. They decided to undertake an exhaustive study of the Bible to prove two points: (1) that Christianity was not a universal religion but limited only to Israel, and (2) that Jesus Christ himself had predicted that Islam would be the only true universal religion.

They read the Bible from cover to cover, carefully and slowly, looking for any errors. They found that Jesus had predicted many future events but never even hinted at either Mohammed or the rise of Islam. Rather than finding glaring mistakes, they instead gained many new insights about God. Moreover, after reading the Gospels, they realized that several passages from their own Koran became much more clear.

Again and again they re-read the Gospels, especially John. One night after studying John, the words of John 14:6 rang like a still small voice in their ears: *"I am the way and the truth and the life. No one comes to the Father except through me."* On their beds they lay awake, pondering its meaning. The next morning they were reading together from John again. When they reached John 3:16, Abdul could no longer keep quiet.

"I am convinced," confessed Abdul boldly, "that Jesus is the true Christ. He spoke to me clearly last night from John 14:6, and this morning we all read the same truth again in John 3:16. I must confess my belief in Him now. He is the true Savior we are looking for. I will embrace Christ and leave behind my old beliefs, whatever the consequences!"

Expecting his two colleagues to denounce him, Abdul paused for a moment. Yet to his amazement, Mohamed and Noor agreed wholeheartedly with him! Their doubts had completely crumbled. All three decided to become Christians! Initially they kept their conversions secret, but in time they submitted a written statement to the Indonesian government detailing the conclusions of their Bible research.

That public confession forever changed their lives. Noor was assassinated by Muslim fanatics for refusing to deny his Christian faith. Mohammed left for the U.S. and chose to remain there permanently, fearing for his safety. Abdul began boldly sharing in public that Indonesians should look to Jesus Christ as their Savior. For his open preaching he was imprisoned numerous times, but many Muslims have come to the Lord through his unstoppable witness.

There are many historical, archeological, and scientific evidences for the truth of the Bible. Yet among the most convincing of evidences are the skeptics who set out to disprove the Bible, only to be won over by it.

"For you have heard of my previous way of life... how intensely I persecuted the church of God and tried to destroy it... But...God...was pleased to reveal his Son in me so that I might preach him among the Gentiles..."

GALATIANS 1:13-16

Lord, I praise You for changing persecutors into preachers. Please continue to use former Muslims like Mohammed and Abdul to spread the gospel among the Muslims.

6
A Martyr's Last Words

IRAN

Alone in his prison cell, Mehdi Dibaj wrote his final defense statement. The Iranian Bible translator was charged with apostasy—abandoning the Muslim faith—a crime punishable by death in Iran. Following are some excerpts from his statement, delivered to the court at his trial.

"I am a Christian, a sinner who believes Jesus has died for my sins on the cross and who, by His resurrection and victory over death, has made me righteous in the presence of the Holy God.

"In response to this kindness, He has asked me to deny myself and be His fully surrendered follower, and not fear people even if they kill my body, but rather rely on the Creator of life, who is the great protector of His beloved ones and their great reward.

"I have been charged with apostasy. In Islamic Law, an apostate is one who does not believe in God, the prophets, or the resurrection of the dead. We Christians believe all three.

"They say, 'You were a Muslim and you have become a Christian.' People choose their religion, but a Christian is chosen by Christ. He says, *You did not choose Me, but I choose you.* People say, 'You were a Muslim from your birth.' God says, *You were a Christian from the beginning.*

"I would rather have the whole world against me, but know that the Almighty God is with me; be called an apostate and be ostracized, but know that I have the approval of the God of glory.

"They tell me, 'Return!' But to whom can I return, from the arms of my God? It is now 45 years that I am walking with the God of miracles, and I feel the warmth of His love in every cell of my body.

"They object to my evangelizing. But 'if you see a blind person near a hole and keep silent, you have sinned.' *(a Persian poem)* It is our religious duty, as long as the door of God's mercy is open, to convince evildoers to turn from their sinful ways and be saved from the coming dreadful punishment.

"I have committed my life into His hands. Life for me is an opportunity to serve Him, and death is a better opportunity to be with Christ. Therefore, I am not only willing to be in prison for the honor of His Holy Name, but am ready to give my life for the sake of Jesus Christ my Lord and enter His kingdom sooner."

In July 1994 Mehdi Dibaj's name was added to the long list of martyrs who determined to die rather than to deny Jesus Christ.

CʒCʒ

"Others were tortured and refused to be released, so that they might gain a better resurrection."

HEBREWS 11:35

Lord, I too look forward to that better resurrection that awaits me. Help me to hold fast to You and not give in to the world.

MEHDI DIBAJ, BIBLE TRANSLATOR, IRAN

7
From Pirate to Fisherman

Without any strength or hope left, Ramonito drifted alone in the ocean on top of a piece of wood. Sensing that death was near, he realized that this was what he deserved for a life of crime.

Ramonito Hetiayon's life quickly spiraled downhill after he was expelled from school. He joined an anti-government outfit and began holding up buses to rob passengers. Later he moved to a new city, where he organized street children into a gang and trained them to be pickpockets. Two prison terms later, he was more ruthless than ever. He joined a gang of fearless pirates who smuggled illegal weapons and drugs in exchange for huge sums of money.

On one particular night, Ramonito's gang was smuggling in a large shipment of guns and drugs. As their speedboats cut through the dark waters, they approached the port cautiously and scanned the shoreline for any sign of movement.

Suddenly bright lights and the roar of heavy engines exploded out of the darkness! Ships from the Philippine Navy had been lying in wait for an ambush! As gunfire began to rain down upon the startled gang, Ramonito immediately jumped overboard into the murky waters. While he was swimming away desperate to save his own life, the rest of his gang were shot dead one by one.

In the darkness, Ramonito managed to grab hold of a piece of floating wood. When dawn broke, he realized that he was the only one who had survived. Exhausted, parched, and despairing of life, he passed out.

After many hours he awoke to find himself being cared for by a couple of sea gypsies, who had found his half-dead body and had nursed him back to health. Ramonito then realized that it was not luck that had saved him but rather God, from whom he had strayed far for many years. Recalling the lessons he had learned in church as a child, he asked God to forgive him and vowed to change his life. Back on shore, he surrendered himself to the police and was sentenced to six years in prison.

This time, Ramonito resolved to leave prison a better man. He realized that God had saved his life for a definite purpose, and he determined to get right with Him so he would not repeat the same mistakes again. While in prison he came to fully understand the gospel and accepted Jesus Christ as his Savior. He then grew steadily in the Lord.

After his release, Ramonito joined a local church and eventually began teaching Sunday School. Later he went out as an evangelist, witnessing boldly about the love of Christ which had transformed his own life. In 1985 the Lord led him to begin planting churches among the Muslims of Mindanao island. Through his tireless efforts, eleven churches have been established and many Muslims have put their trust in the Lord.

The Lord truly transformed Ramonito from a pirate into a fisher of men. How has He transformed your life?

"Therefore, if anyone is in Christ, he is a new creation; the old has gone, the new has come!"

2 CORINTHIANS 5:17

Lord, let my life be transformed day by day into something more beautiful for You.

8
The Invisible Man

Suddenly without warning, two armed terrorists burst into Pedro's home.

"Where is that preacher, Camacho?" the terrorists asked him.

Camacho was sitting right next to Pedro. Following his natural reaction, Pedro was about to point to the chair next to him when the Holy Spirit suddenly stopped him. Surely the terrorists knew what Camacho looked like, since he had been on their hit list for some time. Couldn't they see him sitting there right next to him?

Pedro paused for a moment before slowly answering, "Look around and see for yourself."

The terrorists searched the house, looking in closets and under beds. They carefully checked the yard, looking behind bushes and up in the trees. Camacho just sat quietly the whole time, amazed that they could not see him. Finally after a thorough search, one of the terrorists pointed his gun at Pedro and threatened, "Tell Camacho he can't hide forever. Sooner or later we'll find him, and then he will die!"

That happened in the early 1990s. Today Camacho continues to work as an evangelist. He will never forget the day God spared his life, making him invisible to his enemies.

From 1980 to 1993, radical Maoist groups such as the Shining Path waged a war of brutal terrorism in Peru. Because Christians spoke out boldly against the merciless killings, the terrorists turned against them. Hundreds of Christian leaders died as martyrs for the gospel. But when God had further plans for those targeted for murder, he miraculously protected them. There were times when the terrorists' guns would not fire and times when their knives would not cut. And one time when Camacho was made invisible.

Why did God provide escape for some, while allowing others to be martyred? Why did He send an angel to rescue Peter from prison but allow Stephen to be stoned? There are no simple answers. One thing is certain, however: God has a unique plan for each of His children, and not even His greatest enemy can interfere with His perfect will.

☙❧

"Oh, the depth of the riches of the wisdom and knowledge of God! How unsearchable his judgments, and his paths beyond tracing out!"

ROMANS 11:33

Lord, I cannot always understand Your mysterious ways. Help me to have faith in Your goodness and Your perfect will through it all.

9
Out of the Pit

Augustina had faced many trials in her life, but none were as foul as this one.

The sky was darkening with rain clouds as Augustina rushed outside to bring in her hanging laundry. One by one she collected the shirts and skirts in her arms.

One of the garments had been blown down by the wind, so Augustina stepped atop a concrete slab to pick it up. Suddenly without any warning, the slab cracked and gave way. Unfortunately, it happened to be the slab that covered the sewage pit!

With only enough time to shout "Jesus!" Augustina was sucked down helplessly into the overpowering muck and mire. There was nothing she could do as she sank deeper and deeper. The foul-smelling soup of excrement quickly engulfed her body, and soon she disappeared from sight.

The onlookers were so shocked at the sight of Augustina disappearing into the pit that initially they could only stare in disbelief. Finally one man frantically shouted, "Sister, Sister, where are you?" Augustina heard his voice from the bottom of the pit, but she could neither answer him nor do anything to help herself.

That same day during her morning quiet time, Augustina had been deeply impressed by the words of Psalm 23: *"Even though I walk through the valley of the shadow of death, I will fear no evil, for you are with me."* Yet how could she remain fearless now, knowing that her life would be over in a matter of minutes?

Suddenly she felt a hand beneath her feet pushing her upward. Slowly and steadily, the mysterious hand kept pushing her up higher and higher. When her head finally emerged from the sewage pit, the surprised onlookers rushed forward to pull her out.

They immediately rinsed her off and asked, "Sister, how in the world did you come up?" For not only had Augustina herself come up, but everything else that she had taken down with her—her handbag, the towels, and the clothing—had also come up with her.

Still stunned by the incident, Augustina replied, "Who else could it be but the hand of my Lord Jesus? I have no doubt that it was Him!"

Everyone joined Augustina in praising the Lord for delivering her from the mire!

❧❧

"He lifted me out of the slimy pit, out of the mud and mire; he set my feet on a rock and gave me a firm place to stand. He put a new song in my mouth, a hymn of praise to our God. Many will see and fear and put their trust in the Lord."

PSALM 40:2-3

Lord, thank you for lifting me up out of the pit! There is no other God like you!

10
Happy Steps

What's a man supposed to do when he wants to go for Sunday worship but can't find a single church in town?

It was bright sunny morning. As K.G. Easo put on a freshly pressed shirt, he hummed a gospel melody. He was filled with excitement: this was his first week in his new home in northern India. He could hardly wait to find a church and meet his new Christian family.

Having grown up in a Christian region of southern India, K.G. had been following the Lord since he was twelve. All through his high school and college years he had been actively involved in church. After finishing college with a degree in civil engineering, he was offered an attractive government post in northern India. His move north and his first days on the job had gone very smoothly.

Off he went that day, filled with anticipation as he started down the street looking for a church. Not finding one, he went down another street, and then another. "Where are all the churches in this town?" he wondered. He stopped several people and asked them, but no one knew what he was talking about. After a few more inquiries, K.G. learned that there was not a single church in either that district or the neighboring one. Could it really be that among 4,500 villages there was not even a single church?

Soon K.G. sensed the Lord speaking to his heart: *"You thought you were coming here to work a government job, but I have other plans for you. I have brought you here to be a light to these people walking in darkness."*

39

K.G. had never been to seminary, nor did he know anything about church planting. He only knew how to pray and how to love. He began inviting people into his home for meals. As he gained their trust, he started to share the gospel with them. Before long he was leading a small house church that kept on growing.

More than thirty years later, K.G. has helped plant over 80 churches, baptized 3,500 new believers, opened a Bible school, started an orphanage, and established a Christian elementary school.

All this from a man who thought he was moving up north to take a government job!

CB CR

"In his heart a man plans his course, but the Lord determines his steps."

PROVERBS 16:9

Lord, have I been walking according to my own plan instead of Yours? If so, please redirect my steps so that my life may bear fruit for You.

K.G. EASO, FOUNDER-DIRECTOR OF
SOUL WINNERS INDIA, INDIA

11
Burning the Holy Books

Azali had never tried to set the Koran on fire, so he was quite nervous. *It's not going to burn*, he assured himself. *I know the Koran is indestructible!*

For months, the high schooler in Pakistan had been impatiently listening to his two Christian friends talk about the Bible. Though he had often tried to explain how it was full of errors (as every good Muslim is taught that the Bible is full of errors), he failed to convince them. They kept thinking foolishly that their Bible was the Word of God.

One day an idea came to him: *he would prove the superiority of the Koran over the Bible by setting them both aflame.* He knew the Koran was clearly indestructible—a fact he'd heard all his life—so he was confident he would finally win over his rivals. To his surprise, his two Christian friends agreed to the challenge.

All nerves were on edge as the teenage boys took out both holy books in front of a half-curious, half-uneasy crowd. An awkward hush settled over the group as Azali struck a match and brought it near the Koran. To his utter shock, it ignited! The flames quickly devoured the book, leaving behind only a few charred fragments. Determined not to lose face, he immediately tried to set his friend's Bible on fire. Despite repeated attempts, however, it would not ignite.

Azali initially burned with anger and shame, as he was humiliated before his friends. But later, his emotions gradually melted into curiosity: *if the Bible is really the more powerful book, then what's it all about?* Secretly he began to read it—and its message eventually convicted his heart. Before long he surrendered his life to Jesus Christ and was baptized!

Throughout the Muslim world, many Muslims like Azali have become Christians simply through reading the Bible—once they manage to lay hold of a copy. (Bibles are in short supply across much of the Muslim world.) Let us never take lightly the power of God's Word to transform human hearts!

ՑՑ

"The grass withers and the flowers fall, but the word of our God stands forever."

ISAIAH 40:8

Lord, I praise you for your everlasting, eternal Word which will outlive everything else in this world!

12
No More Fear

M anju used to ask her family many questions, but there was one particular question that she dared not ask. For what would they think of her?

Growing up in a conservative Hindu village, Manju worshipped idols along with the rest of her family. But a day came when she realized that these idols had no life or power. They were simply man-made objects of wood, bronze, or straw covered with mud plaster. They could neither talk, hear, nor see.

"Since this is the case, then why does everyone still worship them?" Manju began wondering. *"Don't they know that idols can't do anything?"* But she was too afraid to discuss this with her family.

One day Manju found a gospel tract describing a living God named Jesus. Curious to learn more, she decided to attend some local classes taught by His followers. Through these Bible studies she learned that unlike the lifeless gods she had been worshipping since childhood, Jesus was actually alive! Not only that, but Jesus loved people so much that He came to earth to save them from hell. After two months of Bible studies, Manju decided to receive Jesus as her Lord and Savior and was baptized.

When her parents discovered that their daughter had become a Christian, they were furious. Immediately they threw her out of the house. Manju was frightened: with no place to stay and no source of income, how would she survive? She cried out to her living God, and He calmed her fears and wondrously provided all her needs.

Manju's new faith was tested again and again. For example, her neighbors threatened to kill her unless she renounced her Christian beliefs. She kept on refusing to do so, so one day they poisoned her drinking water. Manju nearly died, but she was rushed to the hospital and her life was miraculously spared.

In spite of all kinds of hardships and persecution, Manju is still serving the Lord as an evangelist in Bangladesh, pleading with others to turn away from idols and turn to the living God. She plainly declares, "I am so happy that I got the chance to know the love of Jesus, who saved me from my sin. Now I am not scared of whatever happens to me!"

Because of the transforming power of the gospel, this woman who used to be so afraid of others now fears no one but God alone. Has the gospel wrought the same transformation in your life?

C3CR

"Do not be afraid of those who kill the body but cannot kill the soul. Rather, be afraid of the One who can destroy both soul and body in hell."

MATTHEW 10:28

Lord, in my foolishness I am sometimes afraid of what people think. Help me to fear no one but You.

13
The Power of Forgiveness

How could the Lord expect Sunee to forgive her husband? Didn't He know what he had done to her?

Sunee's past life was a string of bad decisions. Marrying her first husband and having a child by him was a big mistake. Then thinking that another man would solve her problems, she gave away her little daughter and got married a second time. But the second husband proved to be worse than the first. Prone to fits of violence, one day he stabbed her in the neck and left her for dead. She survived only because someone found her lying in a pool of blood and rushed her to the hospital.

During her rehabilitation, two of her physical therapists shared the gospel with her. Though Sunee had been a Buddhist all her life, she was so touched by what she heard that she decided to become a Christian.

As she grew in her faith, she learned that one of the key tests of true Christianity is whether or not a person can forgive his enemies. At first she found this teaching too difficult to obey, as she could not bring herself to forgive her husband. But as she continued to grow in the Lord, she knew He was calling her to completely obey Him.

After much prayer, Sunee decided to visit her ex-husband, who was by then in prison. When she arrived there, he was completely shocked to see her alive and well! Sunee explained to him how the Lord had saved her and had completely changed her life. Every week she went to visit him, bringing him gifts of food to supplement his meager prison rations. Through her witness he almost became a Christian, but unfortunately he was transferred to another location before she could lead him to the Lord.

Sunee then set out to reconcile with her daughter Oh, whom she had given away years ago. Oh was filled with bitterness against her mother for abandoning her, and initially she did not want to have anything to do with her. But church members began reaching out to Oh, and in time she also became a Christian.

As Oh grew in her faith, she also learned that she had to forgive those who had hurt her. So just as her mother had previously done, Oh also prayed for grace to forgive. The Lord answered her prayer, and today Sunee and Oh enjoy what was unthinkable in years past: a stable mother-daughter relationship.

The Lord always blesses us when we forgive those who have wronged us. Have you forgiven those who have hurt you?

ॐॐ

"For if you forgive men when they sin against you, your heavenly Father will also forgive you. But if you do not forgive men their sins, your Father will not forgive your sins."

MATTHEW 6:14-15

Lord, is there someone who has hurt me whom I have not yet forgiven? Help me to truly forgive that person.

14
Popeye, Come Home

"D addy, when are you coming home to stay? We need you here!"

His daughter's words struck him like a dagger. For years Joshua Operiano had spent more time at sea than on land, working as a sailor. The money was good, and unknown to his family, so was the wild living. As they traveled from port to port, Joshua and his fellow sailors took every opportunity to indulge themselves in wine and women.

Because he remained at sea for months at a time without returning home, he barely knew his family. And during his few days home, he had to cover up his wrongdoing by telling one lie after another. His daughter's words that day—*"Daddy, when are you coming home to stay?"*—suddenly made him realize what kind of a father and husband he had been. He assured them that he would work for just one more year and then return home for good.

Before long he was called up again to join the same ship. Though he hesitated at first, knowing full well that he would again succumb to the same temptations, he still decided to go. Weakly admitting to himself that his flesh was stronger than his spirit, he prayed a simple prayer on his way out: *"Lord, please help me to change my life."*

Joshua boarded the ship and the vessel set sail for Canada. By the time the ship landed there, Joshua had long since forgotten about his prayer. A good time in the city's red-light district was all he could think about.

Upon arrival he met a port missionary who invited him to a prayer meeting. Joshua had never heard of a prayer meeting, so out of curiosity he agreed to attend. As the meeting got under way, though, he began to regret that he hadn't joined his buddies who were going out for a good time.

At first he felt awkward listening to others share their testimonies of how the Lord had changed their lives. But as the meeting continued, Joshua's callous heart began to soften. During the altar call the preacher suddenly thundered, "I know somebody here wants to change his life! Whoever you are, come forward!"

Joshua knew the Lord was speaking directly to him. *"How did the preacher know about my prayer?"* he wondered. Convicted that he needed to repent of his sinful past, he walked down the aisle, knelt at the altar, and asked Jesus to be his Savior.

Joshua could not wait to return home to announce to his family that he was a new man in Christ and that he was home to stay. How thrilled his family was to hear the good news! Today Joshua serves the Lord as a port missionary in Cebu, Philippines, challenging other sailors to "come home" to their waiting Savior.

"When he came to his senses, he said… 'I will set out and go back to my father and say to him: Father, I have sinned against heaven and against you.' So he got up and went to his father. But while he was still a long way off, his father saw him and was filled with compassion for him; he ran to his son, threw his arms around him and kissed him."

LUKE 15:17-20

Lord, please lead me to someone who needs to come home to You, and give me a chance to show him the way.

JOSHUA OPERIANO, PORT MISSIONARY WITH SEAMEN'S CHRISTIAN FRIEND SOCIETY, PHILIPPINES, WITH HIS WIFE OFELIA

15
Uncovering the Cover-Up

If he kept his mouth shut, he stood a chance of walking free one day. But if he openly confessed the truth, he knew he would have to spend the rest of his life behind bars. What should he do?

Samson used to enjoy a prestigious career in the Philippine Army. But everything changed when he was implicated in a murder case. In fact, Samson had committed the murder himself, but he covered up the truth by falsely accusing two others of joining him. All three were sentenced to life in prison.

While serving his jail sentence, he became bored and restless with nothing to do. To pass the time, he started attending a Bible study conducted by Joshua Operiano, the prison chaplain. One day Joshua was teaching on the Ten Commandments, and Samson's heart began to burn when he heard the commandments, *"You shall not murder"* and *"You shall not give false testimony."*

He returned to his cell and thought deeply about what he had just heard. He realized that he had broken both commandments: first he had murdered, and second he had given false testimony against two others. For the first time in his life, he clearly understood how sinful he was. Stricken with guilt, he prayed to the Lord to forgive him of all his sins. After he had finished praying, he felt a peace in his heart that he had never before experienced.

As Samson continued to attend the Bible study and grow in his faith, he realized that the Lord wanted him to right the wrongs he had committed against the other two suspects. He knew that if he spoke the truth, he would be shutting the door on any future hope of enjoying life outside prison. But he also knew that unless he obeyed the Lord, he would have no peace in his heart.

To everyone's amazement, Samson requested his lawyer to re-open the case so that he could testify before the judge that he had lied about the involvement of the other two suspects. His lawyer was taken aback, but Samson replied, "I am happy to receive even three life sentences, because I have found a joy and a freedom inside these prison walls that no one can take away."

Samson understood that it is far better to live righteously and transparently before God than to enjoy worldly benefits at the expense of disobeying God. For what good does it profit a man to gain freedom, wealth, a good reputation, and/or a job promotion—only to lose his soul in the end?

CƐCƐ

"Better a little with righteousness than much gain with injustice."
PROVERBS 16:8

Lord, please convict me whenever I am tempted to trade my integrity for personal gain.

16
God's Hidden Plan

U nable to have children of their own, Carmen and her husband adopted a baby girl from Honduras. Michelle was a beautiful child, and Carmen loved her the moment she set eyes on her.

After some months Carmen noticed a problem: Michelle did not react when others called out to her. Suspecting something was wrong, she brought Michelle to the doctor. Carmen was devastated by the diagnosis: her baby girl was deaf!

"Lord, how could this happen?" With great faith and persistence she kept on praying, *"God, please heal my baby girl!"*

As Carmen sought the Lord, one day a verse of Scripture leaped out at her: *"Who gave man his mouth? Who makes him deaf or mute? Who gives him sight or makes him blind? Is it not I, the Lord?"* (Exodus 4:11) Convinced that Michelle's deafness was part of the Lord's perfect plan, Carmen was finally able to rest in peace. She began learning sign language to communicate with her daughter. Years would pass by before she would understand why the Lord allowed this apparent tragedy to happen for His glory.

In 1989 on a mission trip to Honduras, Carmen came across a ten-year-old deaf boy. She tried to converse with him, but he knew no sign language as there was no one to teach him. Later during the trip she met a deaf girl the same age as her daughter, who also did not know how to communicate. Carmen was deeply moved with compassion for these children. That night as she prayed for them, the Lord burdened her heart to start a school for deaf children in Honduras.

Carmen had no idea how to go about doing this, especially in a foreign country. But as she committed the work to the Lord, the pieces started to fall into place. From all sides people began donating equipment for the school: books, desks, tools for a wood shop, sewing machines, and chairs. Taking a big step of faith, she rented a building for the school in the capital city of Tegucigalpa.

In the fall of 1989 Carmen opened Love in Action School with 40 deaf students. Since that time, the school has been teaching children sign language plus basic reading, writing, and math skills, as well as a vocational trade such as upholstery, sewing, or cosmetology. The school also clearly presents the gospel, and many students and family members have accepted Jesus Christ through its ministry.

Many of us like Carmen face trials in our lives that seem difficult or even unfair, and we may be tempted to question God's goodness when He fails to answer our prayers in the way we expect. Yet Carmen's testimony clearly demonstrates that whatever the hardship we may be facing, if we simply trust in the Lord, He will surely cause all things to work together for our good and for His glory.

☙❧

"And we know that in all things God works for the good of those who love him, who have been called according to his purpose."

ROMANS 8:28

Lord, help me to trust that You have a purpose for every trial in my life. In Your time, please let me see the good You are working through it all.

CARMEN LINDER, FOUNDER-DIRECTOR OF LOVE IN ACTION
SCHOOL, HONDURAS, WITH HER DAUGHTER MICHELLE

17
Nameless No More

HONDURAS

He didn't know his own name. He didn't know how to ask if anyone else did. And even if someone were to tell him, he wouldn't have been able to hear it.

He was deaf, mute, and—by age three—abandoned by his own mother.

Day after day, the little boy roamed the streets with the other homeless children, sifting through rubbish for something to ease the hunger in his stomach. Somehow he managed to survive.

There were many street children in Honduras, but this little deaf boy caught one man's attention. He heard a radio announcement about Love in Action School for the Deaf and decided to bring this boy there, who was then around ten years old.

During his enrollment, the school director gave him a name—Tito—and made up a birth date for him. Tito was placed in the first grade, and the teachers began the difficult task of teaching him how to communicate via sign language.

At first Tito was shy and withdrawn. But as he learned how to communicate, he became very outgoing. As the school has no dormitories, Tito stayed with another student's family. The school provides him with one good meal every day while teaching him how to read, write, and do basic math. He is also being trained in upholstery. When he graduates, the school will help him get a job at a local furniture plant.

At school Tito learned about Jesus Christ, and his teachers prayed with him every day. As he came to understand the gospel, he gladly accepted Jesus as his Lord and Savior.

Only time will tell what will become of Tito. He may become a powerful witness to the deaf in nearby towns and villages. Or perhaps he will return to teach at Love in Action School. Whatever he does, the fruit he bears will be the direct result of one man who noticed a silent, nameless boy and was moved to compassion.

ങ്ങ

"When he saw the crowds, he had compassion on them, because they were harassed and helpless, like sheep without a shepherd."

MATTHEW 9:36

Lord, would you fill me with compassion and use me to gather some wandering sheep into Your fold?

18
Waking People in Koma

NIGERIA

Who would dare go and share the gospel with those cannibals?

The people living in the Koma Mountains of Nigeria were rumored to be hostile cannibals. Their women were reported to wear leaves, not clothes. But no one really knew anything about them, as they never left their secluded mountain villages.

In 1983 a Nigerian government employee named Gabriel Barau left his job to obey the call of God to reach the Koma tribals. After traveling into the Koma hills, he and his fellow missionaries first built a house to serve as their mission base. The Koma villagers ironically thought that these missionaries were cannibals and assumed that their new building would be used to store the dead bodies of Koma villagers so they could eat them gradually over time! Eventually both groups learned to their relief that neither side practiced cannibalism.

Initially Gabriel and his co-workers encountered great resistance from the tribals because they told their children not to trust the newcomers. But as time passed, the Koma people began to see that the missionaries had come only to help them, not hurt them. Gradually the Lord began opening doors for Gabriel to tell the Koma about the God who made heaven and earth and who died for their sins. In time, the Koma people accepted the message of the gospel and were saved.

Within four years, the Lord had blessed the missionaries with 17 churches planted throughout the Koma hills, each one headed by a

61

Koma pastor. In addition, Gabriel and his fellow workers opened up a school for the Koma children and started adult education classes in the local churches to teach the Koma believers how to read and write. The gospel has truly transformed the lives of these once primitive tribals.

For centuries these people had been living in a spiritual coma. Thanks to the obedience of one man who surrendered himself to the call of God, they have woken up!

৪৪

"Arise, shine, for your light has come, and the glory of the Lord rises upon you."

ISAIAH 60:1

Thank you, Lord, for sending Gabriel to awaken the Koma people. Would You show me a spiritually sleeping friend whom I can help wake up?

19
Special Delivery

L illy desperately wanted to have a baby, but all the doctors told her that it would be impossible. Would the Lord intervene on her behalf?

Lilly had become a Christian just a few months before her marriage to P.G. Vargis. Although he was a hard-core atheist, she initially hoped to persuade him to join her in becoming a Christian. But P.G. had no interest in her religion, and as time went by she lost hope that he would ever change.

Three years into their marriage, Lilly conceived but had a miscarriage. Without giving her any explanation, the doctor simply warned her against ever getting pregnant again. Curious to know why, she consulted three different gynecologists. All of them said the same thing: she could never become a mother. They cited four reasons: (1) her uterus was abnormally small, (2) it was too delicate, (3) it had an odd tilt, and (4) her blood Rh factor was opposite her husband's. Lilly was devastated by the news. In India, a barren womb was considered by society as shameful and accursed.

One day a Christian lady visited her home. While talking with Lilly she said, "Our God is a God of impossibilities! If you just believe, you will see the glory of God!" After she left, Lilly pondered over what she had just heard. Could the God of impossibilities give her a baby despite the doctors' diagnosis? In simple faith she decided to trust the Lord for a baby.

Before long she conceived again. Lilly knew in her heart that the Lord had answered her prayer, but she didn't tell her husband for fear that he would ridicule her. When she went in for her medical check-up, the doctor just shook his head and predicted that within three months she would have a miscarriage. But as the days passed and the pregnancy continued to progress normally, the doctor extended the doomsday to the fifth month, and then to the seventh month. When nothing happened still, he announced that the baby would be definitely born dead. Lilly just listened to him quietly and continued to put her trust in the Lord.

Meanwhile, she managed to persuade her husband to go along with her to an evangelistic meeting. P.G. agreed to go reluctantly, only because the doctor had advised him to keep his wife happy during her pregnancy. The meetings lasted for several days, and by the end of the crusade P.G. had received Jesus Christ as his Lord and Savior! Lilly was ecstatic. The Lord had finally answered her prayers for her husband's salvation.

Finally, Lilly was admitted to the hospital with labor pains. She went in still believing that the Lord would give her a healthy child, but P.G. was expecting a stillborn baby. In keeping with hospital regulations, he had to wait outside the operating room until after the delivery was over. When the nurse came to tell him that everything was over, he rushed in apprehensively and saw his wife lying there, completely exhausted. Drawing close to her side he said, "Don't worry, Lilly. God will give us another child some day."

Lilly just laughed and answered, "But don't you see? He has already given us a healthy baby boy!"

"Sarah said, 'God has brought me laughter, and everyone who hears about this will laugh with me.' And she added, 'Who would have said to Abraham that Sarah would nurse children?'"

GENESIS 21:6-7

Lord, I praise You for being the God of impossibilities. Would You give me faith to trust You more?

P.G. VARGIS, FOUNDER-DIRECTOR OF INDIAN
EVANGELICAL TEAM, INDIA, WITH HIS WIFE LILLY

20
There Was a Christmas

It was Christmas season in the Himalayas, the highest and grandest mountain range in the world. P.G. Vargis and his wife Lilly were taking one of their customary evening walks outside the army station in Kashmir where he was posted. Before them stood the majestic Himalayas. In the deep silence, they sensed the Lord's presence amidst His awesome creation.

As they were worshipping and praying, their eyes caught sight of little cooking fires dotting the hillsides in the distance.

"Lilly," said P.G. excitedly, "stop praying for a moment! Do you see those fires? There must be seventy of them we can see from here, and for every fire there is a family of at least five, seven, or ten people!"

She looked puzzled. "We see those fires every day."

"We are going to celebrate Christmas next week," he continued, "but the people there on those mountains have never even heard that there was a Christmas! Why don't we go and tell them?"

Lilly became unsettled. "But I don't want us to become missionaries! I was trained to be a teacher, and that's what I want to do!"

He replied, "Lilly, I heard the gospel once, and it changed my life. Most people in the world have heard it and have been celebrating Christmas for the past two thousand years. Shouldn't those people have the same chance to hear it at least once?"

"But you can't even speak their language!" She thought her husband was out of his mind.

He took her hand and began pleading with her. "Once, Lilly! Let them hear just once!"

After some time, tears came to her eyes. "Yes," she admitted slowly, "they have a right to hear that there was a Christmas. If you decide to go, then I will also join you."

Looking to the mountainside fires that evening, both husband and wife dedicated their lives to bringing the gospel to the unreached masses in India who have never heard that there was a Christmas. Today they lead Indian Evangelical Team, which sends evangelists to every corner of the nation.

Do you also think that every person on earth deserves to hear at least once that there was a Christmas?

ೞಬ

"Today in the town of David a Savior has been born to you; he is Christ the Lord."

LUKE 2:11

Lord, may the gospel travel to every corner of the earth, that all may hear that there was a Christmas.

21
Truly Positive

MYANMAR (BURMA)

How would Jala react to the sudden news that he was diagnosed HIV-positive?

Along with the rest of his drug-using buddies, Jala had been sharing needles for many years. At that time no one in his village knew anything about AIDS, so many drug addicts were unknowingly injecting death into their veins.

After many years of drug abuse, Jala decided to straighten out his life. He applied for admission at the Myanmar Young Crusaders (MYC) drug rehabilitation center, and there he heard for the first time that there was only one permanent cure for his problem: Jesus Christ. Desperately longing to be set free, Jala surrendered his life to Christ. The Lord delivered him from all his addictions, and from then onward Jala's only desire was to serve his new Master.

Jala studied at MYC's Bible College to prepare for future ministry. In his first year, the college staff took a blood sample from him and discovered that he was HIV-positive. But they wisely withheld this information from him, planning instead to wait until he had become more mature in the Lord. Otherwise he would have definitely lacked the wisdom and the strength to handle this terrible news.

Only at his graduation did the MYC director inform Jala that he was HIV-positive. Stunned, Jala was at first devastated. But after thinking and praying about it for some time, he said, "Of course I am sad, but I know that the Lord is with me. As long as the Lord gives me days to live, I want to share the gospel with as many drug addicts as I can."

Since that day, Jala has boldly shared his testimony with thousands of Buddhists across the country, including many drug addicts. Although most who have the AIDS virus are ashamed to let others know about it, Jala is determined to tell others openly about his life, in the hope that others may learn from his mistakes. Speaking in nationwide crusades, he explains how he first contracted HIV through his sin but later contracted love, peace, and joy through Jesus Christ. He even requested MYC to print his testimony inside a special tract for drug addicts.

Because Jala knows his days are numbered, he is determined to make every day count for eternity. But we who are presumably much more healthy than he is—are we as serious about living each day for the Lord?

ॐ

"Teach us to number our days aright, that we may gain a heart of wisdom."

PSALM 90:12

Lord, teach me to live every day as though it were my last day.

22
Out of the Cave

Hidden away from the world's gaze, the Chepang tribals—cave dwellers of the Himalayas—lived a Stone Age existence well into the twentieth century. They wore no clothing, foraged in the jungle for food, and lived in constant terror of the evil spirits. How would they ever hear the gospel?

Habil Praja was born in a cave and grew up fearing the evil spirits like the rest of his tribe. One day a Christian preacher came to his area sharing the gospel, but Habil chased him away with stones. After this his personal life slid downhill, and he started drinking and fighting.

One day while he was reflecting on the downward spiral of his life, he realized that this was divine punishment for stoning God's messenger. Determined to right his wrongs, Habil decided to learn more about that preacher's God and eventually became convicted by the gospel. At the age of 22 he accepted Jesus Christ as his Lord and Savior. Soon afterwards the Lord put a strong burden in his heart to proclaim the Good News that had set him free.

Since 1994 Habil has been serving as a full-time evangelist and pastor among his own Chepang tribe in Nepal. When he became a Christian, there were only two other Chepang believers in his area. For years Habil has been trekking endless kilometers up and down the sun-scorched mountains in thin sandals to share the gospel and to encourage new believers. The Lord has greatly blessed his labors: 75% of the Chepang who live within a five-hour trekking radius of his village have become Christians! Seven churches have been established, and Habil has discipled five men to look after the work in these different places.

Although most of the Chepang in the surrounding villages have turned to the Lord, Habil's work is still far from over. There are still many Chepang living in other wrinkled folds of the Himalayas who have yet to hear the gospel, including some who have not yet even come out of the caves. And because many of the new believers have only recently emerged from a Stone Age lifestyle, they face staggering developmental challenges in the areas of health, education, housing, food, and employment.

The Lord has laid it upon Habil's heart not only to lead his people spiritually but also to improve their social welfare. He administers local public health programs under the guidance of the Nepali government. He also oversees the new Chepang elementary school in his village. Before this school was built, the local children had to walk two to four hours one way up and down mountains and across rivers just to reach the nearest school. The Lord provided Habil some funds to construct a small school building in his village, and today the students who attend there have to trek "only" up to two hours each way to reach school.

The Lord has truly transformed Habil from an illiterate ruffian into a modern-day Moses, who not only leads his people to a right relationship with God but who also cares for their physical needs in the wilderness. Clearly, he is no ordinary senior pastor. Completely uneducated, he relies wholly upon the Lord for wisdom and strength each day to carry out his heavy responsibilities. And those who work with him can easily see the presence of Jesus Christ in his life.

What do people see when they look at your life?

෮෮෮

"When they saw the courage of Peter and John and realized that they were unschooled, ordinary men, they were astonished and they took note that these men had been with Jesus."

ACTS 4:13

Lord, may I also abide in You and walk as You walked, so that others would see You in me.

23
Out of the Killing Fields

S etan was terrified. His captors were forcing him to destroy a statue of the Buddha. How could he strike his own god with a hammer and still live?

Setan Lee grew up under the tutelage of his grandfather, one of Cambodia's leading Buddhist priests. His aim was to see his grandson also become a priest, so he immersed him in Buddhist teaching until Setan left home to study medicine.

But Setan's life changed forever in 1975, when the Marxist maniac Pol Pot and his military regime known as the Khmer Rouge overthrew the Cambodian government. The Khmer Rouge unleashed a four-year reign of terror known to the world as the "Killing Fields." During this period, three million innocent civilians perished at the hands of the Khmer Rouge, either through murder or as victims of torture, starvation, or disease in the concentration camps. Setan's family was not spared: some were murdered instantly, while Setan and others were sent to the concentration camps.

The Khmer Rouge sought to eliminate every trace of religion from the land. They forced Buddhists to destroy their own Buddha statues. When Setan's turn came, he trembled with terror. With shaking hands he picked up the hammer and brought it down on his god. But nothing happened: he saw that it was just stone and cement, and he became greatly confused.

For two years Setan managed to keep his educational and family background hidden from his captors, because he knew that the

Khmer Rouge was targeting the Cambodian elite for execution. But in 1977 they found out the truth about him and immediately rounded him up along with four other inmates to kill them. Moments before his death, he realized that there had to be a God bigger than the Buddha whom he had smashed earlier. He silently prayed, *"Lord of the universe, if You spare my life, then I will be your witness!"*

The soldiers had already killed the other four inmates, leaving Setan for last. As they were about to execute him, the commander suddenly yelled, "Stop!" Mysteriously and without any explanation, he sent Setan back to the camp. At that moment Setan knew that the Lord of the universe had spared his life. But how would he find out who He was?

Two years later, Setan managed to escape from the camp and began fleeing to Thailand, as thousands of other inmates had also done. Along the way he befriended a Christian fugitive, who told him that the Lord of the universe to whom he had prayed two years ago was Jesus Christ. Right then and there, Setan believed in the Lord and accepted Him as his Savior.

Remembering his earlier promise to God to be His witness, Setan that same day led thirty-two other refugees to the Lord. After safely reaching the Thai border and getting processed into a refugee camp, he became an instant preacher. Daily he proclaimed the gospel to thousands of hope-starved refugees. Eventually he became one of the pastors of the 30,000 new believers in the camp. After emigrating to the U.S, he remained there until 1990, when the door to Cambodia was finally re-opened and he could return to his native land as an evangelist. In 1995 he founded Kampuchea (Cambodia) for Christ, whose mission is to evangelize every single province in the country.

Setan Lee never forgot his promise to the Lord to be a grateful witness of His saving power. Do we have the same zeal to tell others about what the Lord has done for us?

೮ওঙ৲

"Come and listen, all you who fear God; let me tell you what he has done for me."

PSALM 66:16

Lord, may I also witness to others with a heart filled with gratefulness for what You have done for me.

SETAN LEE, FOUNDER-DIRECTOR OF KAMPUCHEA FOR CHRIST, CAMBODIA, WITH HIS WIFE RANDA

24
Instant English

S etan was thoroughly frustrated. For many days the Cambodian translators, who were all Buddhists, had been lying to the U.S. Embassy officials every time a Christian came up for review. As a result, many Cambodian Christians were being unfairly denied permission to emigrate. What should he do?

Setan Lee was one of thousands of Cambodian refugees waiting in the Thai refugee camps to be re-settled in a new country. Representatives from different nations, including the U.S., came to conduct interviews with the refugees to determine who qualified for political asylum and could therefore legally emigrate.

The U.S. Embassy workers did not speak Cambodian, so they hired several English-speaking Cambodians to serve as translators. Before anyone could emigrate to the U.S., he had to go through a three-step process. First, the applicant had to sit for an initial background interview. Second, he had to come back after a few weeks for further questioning. Lastly, he had to appear for a third and final interview. But unknown to the U.S. Embassy staff, if at any time during the process the Cambodian translators learned that the applicant was a Christian, they would accuse him of being a traitor (as "all true Cambodians are Buddhists") and throw away his paperwork.

Setan was the leader of the Christian community in the refugee camp. He knew that he had to intervene on behalf of his people, whose lives were at stake because of this discrimination. But what could he do? He did not know English, so he had no way of communicating with the U.S. Embassy staff.

In a desperate bid for guidance, Setan lifted a Bible above his head, opened it, and placed his finger on a verse. His finger landed on Mark 16:17—*"And these signs will accompany those who believe: In my name they will drive out demons; they will speak in new tongues..."* Taking a cue from this verse, Setan asked all the believers to pray for him to learn English. Believing that the Lord would hear their collective cry for deliverance, the Christian refugees fasted and prayed for him for two days.

The next day a man approached Setan and asked him in English, "Would you like to have an English Bible?" The word that came out of his mouth was, "Sure!" He opened the Bible to the Gospel of John and read it through one time. To his amazement, he understood every word perfectly. Within a week he was fluent in English.

Setan knew that the Lord had miraculously given him this gift so he could rescue His people. He went directly to the U.S. Embassy officials and told them about the ongoing discrimination against the Christians. The American officials promptly fired all the former translators and hired a new batch, including Setan. From then onward, the Christian refugees were able to emigrate to the U.S.

Just as in the days of Moses, when the Lord heard the cry of His people and delivered them out of Egypt with signs and wonders, so also today the Lord listens to the cry of His oppressed children around the world and delivers them. The God of the Exodus is still the God of deliverance today!

"Moses answered the people, 'Do not be afraid. Stand firm and you will see the deliverance the Lord will bring you today... The Lord will fight for you; you need only to be still.'"

EXODUS 14:13-14

Lord, I praise You for answering the cry of Your oppressed children.

25
Middleman on Mindanao

During the close of the 16th century, when Spanish conquistadors were conquering the Philippine Islands in the name of Catholicism, there was one island that resisted to the end: Mindanao. There the Spanish conquistadors encountered fierce defenders of Islam, guerilla soldiers who vowed to die rather than surrender. For the next 350 years of Spanish rule in the Philippines, only the Muslims of Mindanao remained unconquered.

That story has continued to repeat itself throughout history whenever outsiders have tried to rule over the Mindanao Muslims. For example, when the Philippines was under American colonial rule, a lone sword-swinging Mindanao rebel could successfully defeat small bands of American soldiers. Even after the Philippines became an independent nation, the Mindanao Muslims have resisted Filipino rule by burning down Catholic villages. Unfortunately, the Catholic majority has retaliated with similar atrocities.

Caught in the middle is a simple, God-fearing man named Pastor Ramon. Like his Master, Ramon began his ministry without a high school diploma. At the age of 19 he was appointed pastor of a small church in a Mindanao village. Amidst constant danger, he has spent fifty years preaching the gospel of peace on this war-torn island. He is hated by Muslims and Catholics alike: by Muslims for his preaching among them, and by Catholics for his outreach to the "Muslim dogs."

The Lord has continued to deliver Ramon from one peril after another. For example, on one occasion his home was surrounded by a band of rebels. To his surprise, militant Muslims came to his aid. On another occasion while traveling to a preaching engagement, his motorcycle ran over a land mine. He was thrown several feet in the air but landed unharmed.

God has honored Ramon's faithful sacrifice and determination by using him to bring many Muslim militants to the feet of the Prince of Peace. Under Ramon's leadership over 200 churches have been organized in Mindanao. Now nearing 70 years of age, Ramon's body is paying the price for many years of toilsome labor—but still he presses on.

"As long as I have strength," he declares, "I am willing to be spent in the work of the Lord. When I see 30 militant Muslims on their knees receiving Christ, how can I consider retiring?"

❧❦

"Therefore I endure everything for the sake of the elect, that they too may obtain the salvation that is in Christ Jesus, with eternal glory."

2 TIMOTHY 2:10

Lord, may I never retire from serving You.

26
No Ordinary Kindergarten

Over and over Bernardo pleaded with the Lord, *"How can I get these Muslims to understand what You've done for them?"*

Bernardo Balayo became a Christian during World War II after he was miraculously healed from malaria, asthma, and bronchitis. The Lord later put a deep burden in his heart for the Muslim tribes of Mindanao Island in the southern Philippines. He spent several years there laboring to share the gospel but saw little fruit. As a result, he prayed for a new approach to demonstrate the love of Christ to them.

Finally a new idea came to him. Bernardo knew that the Muslim parents in Mindanao were not at all happy with the academic standards of the local schools. Perhaps if he could start a high-quality kindergarten, then the parents would send their children there. And perhaps through the school, first the children and then the parents would come to know the love of Jesus Christ.

With little money but great faith, Bernardo opened Jehovah Jireh School in 1966. Fifty-three children signed up for the first kindergarten class, and all were Muslims except for one. The parents were delighted that for the first time they had an excellent and affordable alternative to the low-standard local kindergarten programs. They did not care whether their children were being taught daily Bible lessons, as long as they were getting a top-notch education.

The Lord blessed Jehovah Jireh School in two ways. First, through the various school functions attended by the parents, relatives, and tribal leaders, 73 families decided to follow Jesus Christ and were baptized! Second, the school was so successful that over the years additional grades (up to 12th) were added, one at a time, to supplement the original kindergarten class. In 1978 the school held its first elementary class graduation, and in 1987 the school produced its first batch of high school graduates.

Even today, most of the incoming students continue to be Muslims. Over the course of their schooling, they learn that Jesus Christ is more than just a prophet: He is the only God who can forgive their sins. By the time they graduate, many students will have personally received Jesus Christ as their Lord and Savior and will have become well-grounded in the Christian faith. In fact, many graduates have even gone on to Bible school and then into full-time ministry.

Praise be to God, who took one man's burden and a simple kindergarten class and multiplied it into a new generation of laborers working in the same harvest field!

இ ஃ இ

"Others, like seed sown on good soil, hear the word, accept it, and produce a crop—thirty, sixty, or even a hundred times what was sown."

MARK 4:20

Lord, You have given us so many different ways to present the gospel to others. Please show me the best way to reach those around me.

Bernardo Balayo, Founder-Director of
Jehovah Jireh School, Philippines

27
Hiding Place

H e suddenly awoke from his dream, frightened and restless. Was it simply a nightmare, or was it a warning from the Lord?

It had been a wonderful convention so far. Over 200 Quechua Indians had gathered for the annual church assembly in the town of Villa Rica. The worship was uplifting; the preaching, life-changing.

As the first day ended, the believers left filled with joy, eagerly anticipating the next day. No one seemed overly concerned that the convention was in a terrorist-controlled area. Delegates slept in the homes of local church members, while a dozen ministers retired in the home of the local pastor.

During the night one of them was awakened by a vivid dream: he saw the pastor's house completely encircled by terrorists. Unable to go back to sleep, he felt a prompting in his spirit to get everyone out of the house. He woke up the other pastors and shared his dream with them.

After a time of prayer the leader said, "I believe God wants us to leave this place." The men left the house and climbed a hill overlooking the town. All this time, they were still unaware of the exact reason why they were leaving the midnight comfort of their beds.

Suddenly from their hilltop perch they saw a group of armed men approaching the pastor's house. The beams of their flashlights pierced the night darkness. They surrounded the house and broke down the door. Inside they found the rooms empty, as the targeted Christians had been safely hidden away by the Lord. The terrorists angrily stormed off into the night, having failed to accomplish their mission.

The watching pastors shuddered, knowing that if the Holy Spirit had not awakened them, all of them would have been killed. From their hilltop hideout they gave thanks to their God and Defender.

ෆ෬

"You are my hiding place; you will protect me from trouble and surround me with songs of deliverance."

PSALM 32:7

How many times have you delivered me from danger without my knowing it, Lord? Thank you for Your unseen hand upon my life.

28
Undeserved Favor

Deeply ashamed of his sins, Mohammed could only think of one way to be sure that Allah would allow him to enter paradise on Judgment Day: by converting a few Christians to Islam!

His parents had raised him as a good Muslim. But after moving to France, Mohammed was lured away by the seductive pleasures of his new country. Before long he was not only using drugs but also smuggling them. The money was good, but his soul was restless and filled with guilt.

When his conscience could bear it no longer, Mohammed gave up his sins and recommitted his life to Allah. He began to faithfully attend mosque, pray, and study the Koran. But he still felt that he was not doing enough good works to make up for his past sins. What could he do to make sure that Allah would accept him into paradise?

He finally thought of an idea. Perhaps if he could convince a few Christians to become Muslims, then he could win back Allah's favor.

"But just how do I get a Christian to convert?" he wondered. Mohammed decided to read the Bible first, to get acquainted with the weak points of Christianity.

As he read the Bible, he became fascinated by the life and teachings of Jesus. He discovered that what he had heard about Christianity and the way he had seen it practiced in France was not at all what the Bible taught. He became more and more interested in reading it and hungrier to find out the truth for himself.

The most surprising teaching he found in the Bible was that salvation is a free gift from God which can never be earned. After further study, Mohammed realized that his search was over. No longer would he have to strive to earn God's favor, because it was freely available in Christ. With great joy he accepted Jesus as his Savior, received forgiveness for his sins, and took hold of the promise of eternal life.

Today Mohammed serves as an evangelist in his home country, Algeria, seeking to make known to other Muslims the same undeserved favor he found.

ೞೕೱ

"He saved us, not because of righteous things we had done, but because of his mercy."

TITUS 3:5

Lord, we could do nothing to earn Your favor. Thank you for freely giving us what we did not deserve!

29
Traffic Cop

H e thought he had his life together, when in reality he was headed straight for hell. But this police officer was too busy directing others to think about where he himself was going.

John Kirema seemed to have the picture-perfect life. Born into a Christian family in Kenya, he grew up in a godly home where missionaries were familiar faces and where the Word of God was regularly taught. Well-versed in the Bible as a teenager, he was asked to teach Sunday School at age 15. After high school he headed straight for the police academy, and within a short time he was posted in Nairobi, Kenya as a traffic policeman.

But one critical piece was missing from John's life: he had never personally admitted that he was a sinner who needed Jesus to save him. Without consciously realizing it, he had become so confident in his own goodness as a "Christian" young man that he failed to see himself as a helpless sinner who needed to be saved by grace. Rather, deep down he felt that he was good enough to get into heaven on his own merit.

One day as he stood on a street corner directing traffic, he saw a gospel tract lying on the road and picked it up. He took it home to read, not knowing that it would change his life.

As he read the tract, his eyes were suddenly opened as if a thick veil had just been lifted. He realized that on the outside he appeared to be a Christian, but on the inside he had no personal relationship with Jesus Christ. All of his church involvement and religious activities did not make him a Christian. Only by confessing that he was a sinner and calling out to Jesus would he have true salvation as well as a personal relationship with the Lord.

That night John surrendered his heart to the Lord. The next morning he awoke with a new joy and a new love for people. He began excitedly telling others what the Lord had done for him. He started a Bible study among his fellow police officers and many of them accepted the Lord. The burning desire to witness to others grew steadily, and within a year he resigned from the police department and enrolled himself in Bible school.

John Kirema eventually founded Cornerstone Evangelistic Ministries, which brings the gospel to the unreached masses in East Africa. Through this ministry 55 churches have been established and thousands have been won to the Lord.

Praise be to God, who stirred an overconfident traffic cop to examine his own heart to see whether or not he was headed in the right direction!

"For it is by grace you have been saved, through faith—and this not from yourselves, it is the gift of God—not by works, so that no one can boast."

EPHESIANS 2:8-9

Lord, am I putting my confidence in my own goodness instead of in Your finished work on the cross? If so, please show me before it is too late.

JOHN KIREMA, FOUNDER OF CORNERSTONE
EVANGELISTIC MINISTRIES, KENYA

30
White-Hot Coals

INDIA

All the villagers trembled as Sandhu stepped atop the white-hot coals with his bare feet. How long would he be able to endure the searing heat?

As more and more villagers in Koralugo turned from their traditional Hindu gods to worship Jesus Christ, the village leader felt increasingly threatened. One day he called his henchmen together and planned a campaign of persecution against the Christians, beginning with a villager named Sandhu.

On February 28, 1995, village thugs assaulted Sandhu on the pretext that he had drawn the sign of the cross in a room reserved only for Hindu idol worship. He flatly denied the charge, alleging that they had completely fabricated the story in order to set him up. But the village leader was not satisfied with his response. He demanded that Sandhu be put to a test to determine whether or not he was telling the truth. If he could stand barefoot on white-hot coals for ten minutes without the soles of his feet being burned, then he would be declared innocent. Otherwise, he would be pronounced guilty.

Sandhu knew he was being set up. But to whom could he appeal for justice, when the village leader was himself behind it? He could only plead to his heavenly defender, Jesus Christ, to vindicate him in the presence of his accusers.

97

The whole village gathered to witness the test. On one side stood the Christian believers, who were praying silently for Sandhu. On the other side stood the anti-Christian villagers, who were jeering at him. Everyone squirmed with vicarious pain as he slowly stepped atop the white-hot coals. Would he scream? Would he immediately jump off?

To everyone's amazement, Sandhu stood calmly without even twitching! Only his mouth was moving, for he was praying continuously. The village leader and his henchmen expected Sandhu to yell at any moment. But to their utter surprise, he remained calm for the entire ten minutes.

When he stepped off the coals, the village leader asked Sandhu to show him the soles of his feet. He could not believe what he saw: there was not even a single scratch! The believers praised the God of Shadrach, Meshach, and Abednego for vindicating His servant and delivering their brother from the hands of his enemies. Meanwhile, forty-seven Hindu onlookers were so impressed by the wonder-working power of Sandhu's God that they subsequently received the Lord and were baptized!

When we cry out to the Lord to vindicate His name and His servants in the presence of mockers, He will surely not refuse to answer our prayers.

"O Lord, how many are my foes! How many rise up against me! Many are saying of me, 'God will not deliver him.' But you are a shield around me, O Lord; you bestow glory on me and lift up my head."

PSALM 3:1-3

Lord, whenever I am being mocked and attacked for my faith, please vindicate me in the presence of my enemies.

31
Criminal or Christ?

INDIA

Pema hated Christianity with all his might. When he came across a Bible, he would tear it up and urinate on it. The most zealous Buddhist monk in his monastery, Pema devoted all his energies to spreading the Buddhist faith.

His religious activities came to a halt at the age of 19 when he contracted malaria. Despite good medical care, his condition worsened day by day. He first called upon each of the Buddhist gods to heal him, but to no avail. Then he called upon each of the Hindu gods, but they could not help him either. His health continued to deteriorate, and the doctors finally gave up on him.

Lying on his deathbed, Pema wondered if there were any other gods whom he had not yet called upon for help. He had once heard someone mentioning that Jesus Christ was a god, but he dismissed the idea as a foolish impossibility. He had seen pictures of Jesus hanging like a criminal, and he scoffed at the idea that some people actually held a criminal to be a god.

While thinking about this, he suddenly saw a vision of Jesus hanging on a cross right in front of him. Taken aback, Pema said, "I don't think you are really a god, because you are hanging like a criminal. But if you heal me, then I will believe in you!"

The next day a group of Christians visited the hospital to share and pray with the patients. Nearing death, Pema requested them to pray for him.

Now Pema had not eaten food for several days. But after they had prayed for him, he suddenly felt hungry. Surprised, the doctors gave him some food, assuming that Pema was mistaking his death pains for hunger pains. But day after day both his appetite and his strength increased and his health steadily improved. To the amazement of the hospital staff, within a month he was well enough to be discharged!

Meanwhile, Pema's family was greatly distressed by the news of their son's illness. They had been praying earnestly to their Buddhist gods for his recovery. When he arrived home, his family was stunned to see him completely healed. Overjoyed, they began invoking the Buddhist thanksgiving rituals. But Pema abruptly stopped them all, announcing, "These gods did not help me! I tried them all. It was Jesus who healed me!"

His family was speechless. What had happened to their son? They guessed that he must have fallen in love with one of the Christian nurses in the hospital, hence this unexpected change of heart. But Pema firmly replied, "I have not fallen in love with any nurse! I have fallen in love only with Jesus!"

This was too much for his family to bear. They beat him up, cursed him for disgracing their clan, and threw him out of the village. The Lord gave Pema a new spiritual family, and in time he became an evangelist along the India-Bhutan border.

Though Pema initially found the message of the cross foolish, he was later won over by its power. What effect has the message of the cross had in your life?

"For the message of the cross is foolishness to those who are perishing, but to us who are being saved it is the power of God."

I CORINTHIANS 1:18

Lord, may the message of the cross always humble me, challenge me, and empower me for Christian service.

32
Re-Tying the Knot

S oonthorn's marriage was falling apart. His wife was fed up with his drinking, smoking, and gambling, and she was always quarreling with him over his bad habits. He had had enough of her nagging and was constantly beating her to shut her up. But whenever he was sober enough to think about his family life, he knew he needed help—badly. But from where?

Born into a Buddhist family, Soonthorn was taught that suffering was the natural consequence of a person's bad deeds. He and his family were often sick, and he believed that sickness was the gods' way of punishing people for their sins. He tried his best to live a good life, but he knew that he lacked the strength to do so. As a result, he became gloomy and depressed, thinking that he could only expect more sickness and suffering in life.

To ease his depression, he began drinking and smoking. He knew it was wrong, but he stopped caring about what the Buddha taught because all his years of following the Buddha had made no difference in his life.

Soonthorn then thought that perhaps a new job and a wife would bring him out of his depression. He headed off for the nation's capital city, Bangkok, where he found a job and got married. At first his life improved a little, due to the initial excitement of all the new changes. But as time went on, his wife started arguing with him over his excessive drinking, smoking, and gambling. Irritated, he would beat her in return. Before long their marriage was on the verge of collapse, and Soonthorn was longing to get out of this horrible marital mess.

One day a Christian lady invited both of them to attend a free English class and Bible study at a nearby church. Curious to learn more, they agreed to go. During the Bible study the teacher took Soonthorn aside and shared the gospel with him. As she spoke, Soonthorn realized that every word she was saying applied directly to his own life. He was so convicted that right then and there he prayed to receive Jesus Christ as his Lord and Savior. That same evening his wife, who was listening intently as another teacher explained the gospel, also decided to receive Jesus Christ!

As Soonthorn and his wife grew in their obedience to the Lord, He delivered them from all their ungodly habits. Their marriage was completely transformed, and Soonthorn declared that his love for her had grown so much that he wanted to marry her all over again! Today he serves as the pastor of a large church in Bangkok, leading other Buddhists to the same transforming peace and holiness that only Jesus Christ can give.

ങ്കൢ

"Unless the Lord builds the house, its builders labor in vain."

PSALM 127:1

Lord, help me to submit every aspect of my life to You, that I may also enjoy Your full blessing in every area of my life.

SOONTHORN KHAMMA, PASTOR-EVANGELIST WITH THAILAND
SOWERS AND REAPERS, THAILAND, WITH HIS FATHER

33
Changed for Good

INDONESIA

Tutik had given up on her husband, Otonus. No matter how many times she had pleaded with him to leave the street gangs, he would never listen. Now he was sentenced to seven months in prison, leaving her alone to raise their little daughter. Having lost hope that he would ever change, she braced herself for the difficult days ahead.

One day after many months, Tutik was busy at home when Otonus suddenly burst through the door. His prison term was over, he said, and he had exciting news to tell.

"I've become a Christian now, and my whole life is changed!" he announced with a wide grin.

While his family listened in disbelief, Otonus shared how he had decided to receive Jesus as his Savior during one of the chapel services in prison. He further explained that he had repented of his former sins and was now living a brand new life. But Tutik just dismissed his claims as a passing phase, for she knew how unstable her husband was. She thought to herself, *"I doubt anything has changed, but time will tell."*

She was surprised to see him praying to the Lord for a job. Was this really the same husband—a former good-for-nothing ruffian— now pleading to God for a job? She could barely hide her amazement when he actually got a job as a taxi driver and began earning a regular income for the family.

Virtually all the taxi drivers were dishonest and rigged their meters to show higher fares. But Otonus refused to rig his meter. When the other taxi drivers questioned him about this, he plainly answered, "I'm a Christian now, and the Lord has changed my life. I don't cheat anymore." His friends ridiculed him, but still he refused to compromise. As the days went by, he started to earn more and more respect from his fellow taxi drivers as well as from his family.

Seeing all this, Tutik could no longer deny that her husband had truly changed for good. So one day she challenged him, "If your Jesus really is the true God, then tell Him to appear to me tonight during my prayer time. Then I will also put my trust in Him!"

That day Otonus prayed fervently for his wife, because he desperately wanted her to know the same peace and joy he had found. That night while she was praying, she suddenly saw a bright light and heard a strange voice saying, *"I am the way and the truth and the life. No one comes to the Father except through me."*

Early the next morning, Tutik told Tonus as he was heading out, "From now on, I will worship your God, Jesus Christ. And I will start going to church with you, and we will take our daughter along with us too!" Otonus was overwhelmed by the Lord's goodness to him, realizing that God had indeed honored his obedience.

Are you also living in such a way that others will be won to Christ by your actions?

"Let your light shine before men, that they may see your good deeds and praise your Father in heaven."

MATTHEW 5:16

Lord, let me live in such a way that others will also desire to follow You.

34
Chosen in Love

INDIA

H is father named him Sangay Hishey, meaning "Omniscient Buddha." Gazing at his newborn son, he dreamed that one day Sangay would follow in his footsteps and become a Tibetan Buddhist monk.

From his childhood Sangay memorized the Tibetan Buddhist Scriptures. He offered holy water and incense daily to the household gods. Yet as he grew older, Sangay knew deep down that he would not make a good monk. The very sight of the Tibetan idols frightened him: big eyes, angry faces, and daggers in hand. How could he help other Buddhists when he himself was terrified by the gods?

To help pay for his college education, Sangay took a job as a proofreader in a print shop. The owner was a Christian, and much of his business came from printing Christian publications. One day Sangay was proofreading an article on the subject of what it means to have a personal relationship with Jesus Christ. He found the contents strange, because he was taught to believe that the gods were evil spirits to be appeased, not friendly beings with whom to have a personal relationship. But he dismissed these thoughts and moved on to the next article, not realizing that a seed had been planted in his heart.

After graduating from college, Sangay began working as a teacher. Some Christians at the school shared with him about Jesus Christ and gave him a Bible to read. At first he was only interested in doing a comparative study of Buddha and Christ. But the more he read, the more he was drawn to Jesus' life and teachings. Jesus spoke of life, joy, and peace with God, in contrast to the fear and gloom in Tibetan Buddhism.

Sangay then read that God did not set out to frighten His children but rather to love them. The words of John 15:16 leaped off the page at him: *"You did not choose me, but I chose you."* All his life he had lived in fear of the Buddhist gods. What a joy it was to learn that Jesus had chosen to love him and save him!

In 1973 Sangay renounced his Buddhist ways and became a follower of Jesus Christ. He changed his name to Stephen as a public sign that he had broken ties with his past. He went on to start a radio ministry which broadcasts the gospel to Tibetan Buddhists across Asia. Through these radio programs, many Tibetans are also coming to personally know the God who died to set them free from fear.

CS CR

"There is no fear in love. But perfect love drives out fear, because fear has to do with punishment. The one who fears is not made perfect in love."

I JOHN 4:18

Lord, please use this radio ministry to liberate Tibetans from their bondage to Satan's fear, so they can worship the Living God.

STEPHEN HISHEY, FOUNDER-DIRECTOR OF
GOOD NEWS FOR TIBET RADIO, INDIA,
TALKING WITH SOME TIBETAN BUDDHIST MONKS

35

Grounded by God

INDIA

Stephen and Susie Hishey were at home one evening when they heard the noise of a large crowd gathering outside. Looking out the window, they saw their neighbor's house jam-packed with people. What was going on?

Stepping out to have a look, the Hisheys discovered that the crowd was watching two men in the center of their neighbor's living room. One was a Tibetan Buddhist priest, and the other was his disciple sitting cross-legged on the floor next to a fire of hot coals. The priest was about to make his disciple levitate through tantric (demonic) powers, and the crowd had gathered to witness this feat.

The priest called upon a spirit and requested it to come and possess his disciple. In a few moments the spirit entered him, and he began flying around the room—still in his cross-legged position. After a while he came down again, grabbed some live coals from the fire, and ate them. Then he began to levitate again.

Alarmed by what he was seeing, Stephen turned to his wife and said, "Let's pray against the power of Satan!"

There in the doorway, the Hisheys asked Jesus Christ to demonstrate His power and His presence. Suddenly the man who was levitating fell straight down to the ground! The crowd began to murmur, wondering how the spirit's power could have suddenly failed. The Buddhist priest and his disciple were both bewildered and embarrassed, completely at a loss to explain what had happened. Only

Stephen and Susie knew that Jesus had once again demonstrated His supremacy over all other gods.

Once we commit our lives to the King of kings and the Lord of lords, we never need to fear any other power, whether heavenly or earthly, visible or invisible.

⊰⊱

"I know that the Lord is great, that our Lord is greater than all gods. The Lord does whatever pleases him, in the heavens and on the earth."

PSALM 135:5-6

Lord, I praise You, for Your name is higher than any other name and Your power greater than any other power in the universe. Let me never fear anyone but You!

36
Harvest at Last

Pastor Miguel's church attendance kept dwindling, and any effort to bring in new people seemed futile.

Knowing that their government opposed religion, Cubans were reluctant to step inside churches. Youth were being indoctrinated with atheism. More and more people were being convinced that the Bible was just a book of myths, full of contradictions.

It was a dark time for the church in Cuba. Fidel Castro's Communist regime had been in place for years. Many ministers were in prison, scores of others had fled the country, and some had even been martyred. Fewer than one in 200 Cubans were genuine followers of Jesus Christ.

In spite of all this, Miguel still continued to preach the gospel while his faithful remnant prayed for the lost in Cuba. More than twenty years went by and church attendance had now dipped below twenty, with the youngest member being over forty years old. Many times Miguel questioned his calling. But whenever he thought about quitting, the Lord would encourage him to remain faithful.

Finally the Lord answered his prayers. It began when a woman, crippled for years, was suddenly healed by the Lord. The news spread like wildfire, and soon people were bringing the sick from afar to be prayed over. Hundreds were healed from diseases ranging from cancer to blindness. In the next few months over 40,000 people passed through the doors of this little church. Some came out of curiosity, but many came out of real spiritual hunger.

Because the majority of these miracles were happening to non-believers, multitudes in the city of Cardenas turned to Jesus Christ. In every church service dozens of people came forward to ask the Lord into their hearts.

During his first 25 years of service, Miguel could count on one hand the number of new believers through his ministry. But since 1987 when the season for harvest finally arrived, thousands have come to the Lord. Under his leadership the church in Cardenas has grown to 17 congregations, each with an average of 150 people. Presently 33 more churches are being planted in surrounding towns.

The season for sowing was long and difficult, but the abundant harvest has made all the labor and tears worthwhile!

ભ્ભભ

"He who goes out weeping, carrying seed to sow, will return with songs of joy, carrying sheaves with him."

PSALM 126:6

Lord, let me also be faithful to sow the Word always, trusting You to bring in the harvest in Your time.

37
Not Far from the Truth

ALGERIA

S alim felt so far from God. One day while coming back home from the mosque he asked himself, *"Where is God, and why do I feel that He never listens to me when I pray?"*

Salim had always been a devout Muslim until he realized one day that God was not answering his prayers. He was soon plagued with all kinds of doubts. "Is there really a God after all? If so, does He really care about me? If not, then why should I keep on attending the mosque?"

Discouraged and directionless, Salim began to drift. First he started drinking alcohol, and then he started using drugs. Eventually he began stealing in order to support his bad habits.

One day Salim came home drunk. He collapsed into bed, switched on the radio to relax, and adjusted the dial until he found a station playing nice music. After some time he realized that it was a Christian broadcast. He listened carefully as the radio preacher delivered a very powerful message on God's love for His children. Despite his drunken state, Salim was deeply touched by the message. At the end of the program he noted down the station address and decided to write them.

To his surprise, they answered his letter with a small package containing several interesting booklets about God. Salim did not know anything about Christianity, nor did he know any Christians, but what he read greatly touched his heart. The radio station offered him a free Bible correspondence course, which he decided to accept.

As the months went by, Salim learned more and more about what the Bible taught. He realized that all the answers to his former questions lay in this book. Most importantly, he learned that God was not far away at all: he simply had to call out to Him in faith, and He promised to come near.

Salim stopped drinking and using drugs, and his former gloomy countenance now glowed with a new zest for life. Within one year of listening to that original radio broadcast, he decided to accept Jesus as his Lord and Savior. He continued to grow alone in his faith for two more years, after which time he finally met some other Algerian believers and then joined them for fellowship.

Salim learned that although God may seem far away, it is only because we have not taken the right steps to approach him: putting our faith in Jesus Christ, confessing and repenting of our sins, and trusting in His promise to remain with us always. Instead of blaming God for the distance, let us remember that He is the one who is always running after us, not the other way around. As someone once quipped: "If God seems far away, then who's the one who moved?"

"Come near to God and he will come near to you."

JAMES 4:8

Lord, whenever I feel far away from You, let me always remember that I'm the one who has moved.

38
Bye-Bye Booze

Isubai was desperate. Ever since the villagers in Uchal started turning to Christ, his liquor sales kept plummeting. Unless things changed, he knew that he would soon be out of business.

Everything was going well for Isubai before the evangelists came to his village. Although the other families were struggling to make ends meet, he had no difficulty earning a healthy income. As owner of the village liquor shop, he knew he could always count on a steady stream of customers.

When the evangelists first arrived and began preaching, Isubai did not care about their activities. After all, what was wrong with adding one more god to the large assortment of Hindu gods? But as time passed and more and more villagers became followers of Jesus, he noticed that they stopped drinking alcohol. As a result, his liquor sales declined sharply.

Desperate to save his business, Isubai started harassing the evangelists to try getting them to leave. But before long, his wife became seriously ill with intestinal swelling. He brought her to all the village doctors and local magicians, but no one could help her.

As a last resort, Isubai asked his wife to go to the church and request prayer for healing. The evangelists and new believers warmly received her and prayed fervently for her. The Lord answered their prayers: she was completely healed! When she returned home, Isubai saw what Jesus had done for her and he was deeply ashamed of his anti-Christian behavior. He humbly confessed his sins and accepted Jesus as his Lord and Savior.

After becoming a Christian, Isubai faced a major dilemma: what should he do about his liquor shop? On the one hand, he knew that his liquor business was displeasing to the Lord. On the other hand, he knew that if he closed down his shop, it would be a huge financial loss for him. After wrestling with this issue for some time, he finally decided to close down his business as a bold act of obedience to the Lord. He now works as a common laborer, earning just a fraction of what he used to make earlier. But his heart is filled with peace now, knowing that the Lord will bless him for choosing God over money.

Isubai's example also challenges us to search our hearts. Are we in any way compromising the Lord's standards in our work and thereby actually serving money instead of God?

∞

"No one can serve two masters. Either he will hate the one and love the other, or he will be devoted to the one and despise the other. You cannot serve both God and Money."

MATTHEW 6:24

Lord, please convict me if I am giving more importance to earning money than to obeying You. Give me the courage to make any necessary adjustments in my life.

39
Through the Flood

INDIA

Afterᵉ the floodwaters had receded, the villagers carefully made their way back home through the debris. Only one question burned in their hearts during the entire journey: would they find anything still standing?

Though floods are common during the yearly monsoon (rainy season) in India, the rains of 1995 ranked among the worst that anyone in the village of Devgarh could ever recall. As the rains kept coming down and the river kept swelling, it became clear to the villagers that they might have to evacuate.

Men labored furiously building barricades to hold back the rising water. Women packed whatever belongings they could carry and gathered their children. As the river began breaking through, the villagers had no choice but to flee to higher ground.

Running for their lives, they managed to escape to a nearby village to wait out the rains. All feared that they would lose everything and have to start all over again. Christians from the church in Devgarh prayed that God would have mercy on them and demonstrate His power through this disaster.

After days of waiting, the rains finally stopped and the waters began to recede. The villagers began returning home, mentally preparing themselves for the sober reality that lay ahead. Rebuilding would not be easy.

When they arrived, their fears were confirmed: many homes had been completely washed away, and those that were still standing had suffered great damage. But as they surveyed the destruction, they saw to their amazement that one building had remained completely intact: the church! Miraculously, it had withstood the raging flood without any damage.

The pastor opened the church doors and called his people together for a time of thanksgiving. The Christians knew that the Lord had answered their prayers, demonstrating His power in front of all the watching villagers by preserving His house. In the weeks that followed, hundreds of new believers were added to the church.

What began as a flood of destruction to the village of Devgarh turned into a flood of blessing to many others.

CﬔCR

"When you pass through the waters, I will be with you; and when you pass through the rivers, they will not sweep over you."

ISAIAH 43:2

Lord, time and time again You have turned my troubles into something beautiful. Thank you for all You have done for me!

40

Courage to Tell

T wo schoolteachers, Tranpui and Indira, were chatting one day during a school break when the conversation suddenly turned serious.

"I love you a lot, Indira. You're a dear friend of mine, but I'm very sad for you."

"What do you mean?" asked Indira curiously.

"You see, Jesus is coming back to earth one day; and when He comes, He will take me up to heaven with Him but you will be left behind!"

Indira found her friend's pronouncement funny. How could Tranpui think that she, coming from a royal Hindu family, would not make it into heaven?

Tranpui tried to explain to her friend that she was a sinner. But Indira protested, "How can I be a sinner? I obey my parents, I don't run around with other guys, and I have faithfully worshipped my gods since I was a child."

"Have you ever told a lie?" Tranpui inquired.

"Well, yes," Indira answered hesitatingly.

"Do you ever get jealous of others?"

Again Indira quietly nodded.

Then Tranpui explained, "You see, the Bible calls all of these behaviors 'sins.' If you've done any one of these things, then you're a sinner."

Indira then asked, "You say that Jesus died for me. But how could he die for me when I wasn't even born yet?"

Tranpui reached out for her long classroom pointer and picked it up from the center. "See? Just now when I picked up this pointer, I picked it up from the center, didn't I? But notice that the whole pointer—from one end to the other—also came up with the center portion. The whole human race is like this pointer. Adam was the first man," she said, pointing to one end of the stick, "and the other end represents the last man to live. Christ died right in the middle," she said, pointing to the center. "When He died, He picked up the sins of the whole human race, from the first man to the last man."

"That makes sense," Indira replied. "But I am a Hindu. We have our own gods."

Tranpui continued, "Imagine that you are lost and have come to an intersection. There are three dead men lying there and one living man. To whom will you ask directions?"

"The living man, of course," replied Indira.

"Don't you see? I'm not saying that your gods are bad gods. They have all done good things. But they all died. Jesus is the only God who died and rose again. Isn't it better to follow a living God than a dead one?"

Troubled by their conversation, Indira went home and prayed alone in her room that night. *"Jesus, for years I had worshipped my own gods but never felt anything from them. If you are really a living God like my friend said, then let me know the difference between worshipping a dead god and a living God!"*

As she prayed, she suddenly felt the presence of the Living God in her room. Overwhelmed by her own sinfulness, she confessed her sins and asked Him to forgive her. From that night onward, she became a passionate follower of Jesus Christ. Eventually the Lord called her to start a ministry to her own Hindu people, through which many former idol worshippers have come to know the Lord.

Indira's fruitful ministry is the direct result of one woman who had the courage to tell a friend about Jesus Christ. Whom will you tell about Him?

ॐॐ

"Go quickly and tell… He has risen from the dead…"

MATTHEW 28:7

Lord, would You give me the courage to tell someone about You?

INDIRA CATHERINE HSU, FOUNDER-DIRECTOR OF
MARANATHA COMPASSION INDIA

41
Refusing to Shut Up

The guards threw him into the prison morgue to die. As he lay among the rotting corpses in the darkness, Prem pleaded with the Lord to take his life. He could no longer bear any more suffering.

Like the rest of his countrymen in Nepal, Prem Pradhan had grown up Hindu. While serving with the British army during World War II, he had heard the gospel and become a Christian. The Lord later called him to return to Nepal and preach the gospel to the millions there who had never heard of the name of Jesus.

Despite stiff government penalties for evangelism, Prem fearlessly proclaimed the gospel in his homeland. In time, many people responded to his message and were baptized. But Prem a steep price: he was arrested and sentenced to six years in prison for evangelizing and baptizing.

In those days, Nepali prisons were literally dungeons of death: twenty-five or thirty people jammed into a tiny cell without any ventilation or bathroom facilities. New inmates often passed out from the horrific stench within minutes of arrival. Prisoners slept on a dirt floor crawling with rats, cockroaches, and lice. They were allotted just one cup of rice per day, and as a result most became severely ill from malnutrition.

Prem's spirit withered upon seeing these conditions. If the Lord had indeed called him to win souls and plant churches, then why did

He let him come here just to rot to death? But the Lord spoke to him: *"I called you to build my church, and you will do it in here too."* After this revelation, Prem began actively sharing the gospel with his fellow inmates. Many put their trust in the Lord, and after being released some went out as evangelists throughout Nepal.

As time passed and the prison authorities saw that the oppressive conditions were not denting Prem's religious enthusiasm, they decided to break his spirit in another way. They chained him hand and foot and threw him into the prison morgue, where the bodies of dead prisoners were kept. The authorities predicted that Prem would last only a few days in there before breaking down.

The space was so small that he could neither stand up nor stretch out. In the darkness he could faintly make out the outlines of the corpses, which were oozing foul-smelling fluids onto the floor beneath his shivering body. Unable to bear his circumstances any longer, Prem begged the Lord to take him home quickly. But again the Lord spoke to him: *"I suffered so much for you. Are you not willing to suffer a little for Me?"*

At this, Prem's heart became lighter, and he began praising the Lord. One day the guard overheard Prem praying and asked him whom he was talking to. Prem answered, "Jesus." Shining his flashlight into the darkness but not seeing anyone, the guard asked Prem where "Jesus" was hiding. Prem then shared the gospel with him, and he also became a believer!

When the prison authorities realized that Prem was leading one person after another to the Lord, they transferred him to another prison. But there he also refused to shut up, so they had to transfer him to yet another place. All together between 1960 and 1975, Prem spent a total of ten years in fourteen different prisons suffering for Christ. As a result of his witness, many in Nepal have become believers in Jesus.

People used to ask Prem why he did not evangelize more discreetly in order to spare himself years of imprisonment. Prem plainly answered, "How can a Christian keep silent? Jesus died openly and publicly for us. If he did not try to hide himself on the cross, then we should also speak out openly and publicly for Him—regardless of the consequences!"

Prem was not ashamed of his Lord, so he refused to shut up. What about you?

CЗCЯ

"Whoever acknowledges me before men, I will also acknowledge him before my Father in heaven. But whoever disowns me before men, I will disown him before my Father in heaven."

MATTHEW 10:32-33

Lord, please convict and change me if I am ever ashamed to tell others about You.

PREM PRADHAN, FOUNDER OF
NEW LIFE MISSION, NEPAL

42
Flight for Life

I t was his last option. He did not want to leave his wife or his five-year-old son. But what choice did he have?

Only a few months earlier, Ali had decided to become a Christian and was baptized. His Muslim wife was initially supportive of his decision and indicated that she would soon follow him in his new faith.

But things did not turn out as Ali had hoped. At that time he was still living with his parents and brothers even after his marriage, according to the joint family system practiced in Bangladesh. One day his wife told his family that Ali had left Islam to become a Christian. They were furious and denounced him as a fool and as an apostate.

Then one day after returning home from church, Ali was beaten up by one of his brothers and warned never to go back again. He refused to listen to the warning. Instead, he fled and took refuge in the church.

After a few days his family went to the church and brought him back home. They ordered him to stop attending church, reading the Bible, or praying to anyone else besides Allah. But although he was afraid of them, he knew that he must only fear the Lord. So he continued to secretly read his Bible and pray after everyone else in his household had gone to sleep.

One night his wife woke up and found him praying. She immediately called one of his brothers and complained to him that Ali had started praying to Jesus again and was disturbing her sleep. Furious, his brother began to beat him.

Ali cried out, saying that he would not give up following Jesus no matter what they said or did. But his family still refused to back down from their demands: no church, no Bible, and no Jesus. Ali then had no choice. The next morning he quietly left home without informing anyone.

We who live in Western countries seldom face the kind of persecution that our brethren in Hindu, Muslim, and Buddhist nations encounter. Let us remember to pray for them, including Ali, that the Lord would show them mercy in their sufferings and change the hearts of their persecutors.

CЗCЯ

"Anyone who loves his father or mother more than me is not worthy of me; anyone who loves his son or daughter more than me is not worthy of me; and anyone who does not take his cross and follow me is not worthy of me."

MATTHEW 10:37-38

Lord, please show mercy to Ali and let him be re-united with his wife and son. Let them also come to know of Your love and salvation.

43
Maid for Glory

Once upon a time, the Lord used a simple maid to launch a full-scale revival among her people.

A poor woman from the Akha tribe in northern Thailand was desperate to earn some extra income for her family. She decided to leave her sleepy mountain village and head south for Bangkok, a huge metropolis where she figured she would surely find work.

After reaching there she got a job working as a maid in a Christian home. A nominal Christian herself, she readily agreed to attend church with her master's family. The regular teaching from God's Word greatly blessed her heart, and before long she was growing strong in her faith.

After some time, she learned that this same church also ran a Bible school for lay people. She thought of her own Akha tribe, which did not have even a single pastor or evangelist, and wondered if she could possibly study at the Bible school herself in order to return back home and minister to her own tribe. True, she had come to Bangkok to earn money for her family. But was the Lord calling her for something else?

She finally shared her burden with her employer, who willingly released her so she could enroll in the Bible school. After completing her studies, she returned to her village as a trained evangelist. Her village leaders were stunned: they never knew any Akhas who had received Christian training! When the Western missionaries who had evangelized them returned home years ago, they left behind no trained Akha pastors, so no one was left to shepherd them.

Knowing their desperate need for pastors and evangelists, the village leaders decided to make a special journey to Bangkok to inquire whether or not this Bible school could train any more Akhas. What a surprise it was for the Bible school directors to one day suddenly find a group of Akha men standing at their door, begging not for money but for Bible training!

That surprise visit led to the creation of the Akha Bible Training Institute, which conducts classes four times a year for Akha men and women. Well-equipped with God's Word now, Akha evangelists are penetrating interior hill regions with the gospel and Akha pastors are shepherding their own growing congregations.

All because a simple housemaid with a burden for her own people stepped out in faith for the Lord!

❧❧

"But God chose the foolish things of the world to shame the wise; God chose the weak things of the world to shame the strong. He chose the lowly things of this world and the despised things—and the things that are not—to nullify the things that are, so that no one may boast before him."

I CORINTHIANS 1:27-29

Lord, I praise You for using the foolish, the weak, and the lowly people of this world to do great things for Your kingdom!

AKHA LADIES SINGING AT CHURCH, THAILAND

44
Prayed Out

A lone in a small cell, Brother Bacong knew that his captors would execute him the next morning. There was nothing he could do to save himself, so he decided to spend the final hours of his life pouring his heart out to the Lord.

The mountains of Negros Oriental, an island in central Philippines, were a hotbed of anti-government unrest in the late 1980s and early 1990s. Communist guerillas roamed the hills, preaching violence and terrifying villagers.

The Lord called Brother Bacong into this area to bring the gospel. He traveled in and out of the mountains without fear, meeting the villagers and sharing the love of Christ with them. Over time his activities generated suspicion among the Communists, who were closely monitoring his movements.

During one of his trips into a remote area, Bacong was suddenly taken prisoner by a band of Communist guerillas. They dragged him to their hideout and accused him of being a spy for the Philippine government. Bacong protested, arguing that he was innocent of such charges, but his plea fell on deaf ears. The commander sentenced him to be executed the following morning.

Thrown into a small cell, Bacong immediately began to pray. He prayed for his wife and children, who would soon be without a husband and a father. He prayed for the Lord to raise up someone else to continue the work of evangelizing these mountain villages.

He prayed for his captors, that the Lord would penetrate their hearts with His love. As he prayed, his prayers turned into praises, and he had a deep assurance that the Lord was with him in his final hour.

Early the next morning, the guerillas opened his cell door and led him out. With the Lord's peace ruling over his heart, Bacong was prepared to face death. His captors brought him to their commander, who was waiting for him.

"We observed you praying last night," the commander said, "and we realized that you are not a spy. We know that no one could pretend to pray with that kind of fervency. You are free to go!"

Bacong was saved by the hand of the God who answers prayer. Have you cried out to him lately?

⋐⋑

"To the Lord I cry aloud, and he answers me from his holy hill."

PSALM 3:4

Lord, thank you for always listening to the sincere and heartfelt cries of Your children.

45
Life in the Slaughterhouse

CUBA

Yolanda risked a prison sentence for what she was doing, but she didn't care.

Just a few weeks ago, she and her companions had been commissioned for the Lord's service. As they stood at the altar, the church leaders laid hands on them and prayed. Their mission: to plant a church in Matanza, a Cuban city whose name means "slaughter."

For many days they went knocking on doors, passing out tracts, and sharing the gospel. Despite the fact that their activities were strictly forbidden by the government, like the New Testament apostles they chose to obey God rather than men.

In each home they visited, they shared that they would soon be starting a house church in that neighborhood. Although many people rejected them, others were very open to their message. After decades of government-enforced atheism, the gospel was truly good news to their ears.

Before long Yolanda had gathered a core group of seekers wanting to study the Bible. Then the Lord answered her prayers by prompting one Cuban couple to open their home for the meetings. There all the seekers met and began singing, praying, and listening to the Word of God. Within a few weeks several families had decided to become Christians! Soon they had to move out living room furniture before each service to make room for extra chairs. One year later, the house church had grown to 60 members and was ready to divide and multiply.

Today there are 25 house churches in Matanza with a combined attendance of over a thousand. Each one is a living testimony that God, through the fearless dedication of His saints, can bring new life even in a "slaughter"-house!

ଓଃଔ

"They will renew the ruined cities that have been devastated for generations."

ISAIAH 61:4

Lord, thank you for continuing to bring new life in spiritual wastelands. Enable Your servants in such places to speak Your Word with great boldness.

46
A Heavy Price

S onia's greatest fear came true: her parents discovered that she
had become a Christian. What would they do to her now?

Born into a Muslim family in North Africa, Sonia moved to
France with her parents. From childhood she had been taught to
stay away from Christians. She never gave a second thought to Christianity until one day at the age of 15 she found herself sitting at a
weekend youth retreat, having been invited by some friends.

At first Sonia just quietly observed the praying and the preaching, all of which were new to her. But during the weekend, she was
struck by the Christians' intimate relationship with their God—
something she had never seen before in her own Muslim community. By the end of the retreat, her heart had been deeply touched.
But after returning home, Sonia tried to shrug it off. *"I am a Muslim
Arab,"* she reminded herself.

Two weeks later, her friends invited her to a church meeting.
While the pastor was speaking, she was caught off guard: he was so
accurately describing the struggle going on in her own soul! *"How
could he know my heart so well?"* she wondered. Back home again she
re-examined her thoughts about God. Her heart wanted to take hold
of the Christian faith, but how could she go against everything she
had been taught since childhood?

Later her friend gave her a copy of the Gospel of Luke. As she
read it, she knew that she could no longer resist the love of God that

had been tugging at her soul for many days. When she reached the end of the booklet and read the sinner's prayer, she prayed it straight from her heart. Immediately she felt a fresh peace deep within.

Sonia began attending church secretly. But one night her parents stopped her on her way out and asked her what she was carrying in her hand. When they saw it was a Bible, they became furious. Forbidding her from ever attending church again, they ordered her to choose between Jesus Christ or her family.

What should she do? As much as she loved her family, Sonia knew that she could not give up her new Savior. With great sadness and fear she gathered her belongings and left home. Forbidden by law to live with Christians as long as she was a minor, Sonia was forced to enter a home for juvenile delinquents. She stayed there for three years, during which time she received many letters of encouragement from Christian friends.

The Lord eventually put a burden in Sonia's heart to reach the lost, so she enrolled in Bible school. Later she started a missionary training school in France, through which over 300 people have been trained to reach North African Muslims with the gospel.

Sonia had to pay a heavy price to follow Jesus, but in return she has gained something that money could never buy: eternal favor in the eyes of the Living God. What price are you willing to pay to follow Him?

"Then Jesus said to his disciples, 'If anyone would come after me, he must deny himself and take up his cross and follow me.'"

MATTHEW 16:24

Lord, may I be willing to pay any price in order to follow You faithfully till the end.

47

The Orphan Who Never Forgot Where He Came From

CHAD

The nearly 50-year-old man they call Bako still weeps at the plight of orphans, because he still remembers the pain of being an orphan himself.

When Bako was just two years old, his father was poisoned by his enemies and his mother died that same year. Little Bako was then taken in by his Christian grandmother. It was a miracle that he even survived, as frail as he was—particularly in a place as bleak and as impoverished as the African desert nation of Chad.

Even more miraculous, however, was how his tender faith in Christ could survive the equally hostile spiritual landscape of Islam. Bako came to Christ at the age of eight and immediately began to share his new faith with others. Shortly after his conversion, however, the orphan boy was sent to live with his uncle, who was hostile to Christianity.

One day his uncle started to beat him violently, because he was furious that his bright nephew was following Christ and planning to "waste" his life as a pastor. But in a remarkable act of respectful defiance, Bako suddenly grabbed his Bible, opened it up, and started reading it to comfort himself—all in the midst of his brutal beating! The specter of a little orphan boy silently reading his Bible even while blows were raining down on his thin body proved too much for his uncle to bear. Both awed and frightened by his nephew's un-flinching commitment, his uncle withdrew his hand. And Bako knew that the Almighty God, the Father of orphans and widows, had successfully defended him at last. Psalm 27:10 became a lifeline of hope: *"Though my father and mother forsake me, the Lord will receive me."*

His uncle finally drove him away because of his faith, but God took care of Bako through the help of compassionate Christians. He eventually completed Bible college and began pastoring, teaching, and leading missions outreach programs in his own country. His humble giftedness as a minister among his own people drew international attention, and in 1998 he was awarded a prestigious Billy Graham scholarship to pursue a Master's Degree at Wheaton College in the U.S. When he returned home to Chad in 2001, he was asked to be the leader of all the evangelical churches and mission agencies in his country—a position he humbly accepted.

But the orphan-turned-national Christian leader who oversees 3,000 churches has never forgotten where he came from. Even as Bako spends his days preaching, training pastors, and deploying evangelists to tough mission fields, his mind wanders back to his days as a lonely orphan boy and grieves over the plight of thousands just like himself. (A staggering half million people—one of out of every twenty people in Chad—are orphans.) Having walked before in their lonely footsteps, he knows their deepest heart cry: for a home of their own, for someone to love them.

For years Bako had dreamed about building a Christian orphan village in Chad—a warm, loving place where orphans like himself could be cared for and nurtured in a godly setting. And by God's grace, Bako's dream is finally coming true. Soon he hopes to have 10 orphan homes completed for 300 of the neediest orphans in Chad. True, it's just a drop in the bucket compared to the total need. But at least 300 potential future Bako's will be saved from the clutches of starvation and despair.

With God's help, Bako has been able to transform his pain—the pain of an extremely dysfunctional childhood—into a fruitful ministry of compassionate outreach to those suffering in the same way he used to suffer. Does the Lord want to do something similar through your life too?

❧❧

"Praise be to the God and Father of our Lord Jesus Christ, the Father of compassion and God of all comfort, who comforts us in all our troubles, so that we can comfort those in any trouble with the comfort we ourselves have received from God."

2 CORINTHIANS 1:3-4

Lord, please let me never forget from where You brought me, so that I can be useful in reaching out to others still trapped in that same place.

NGARNDEYE BAKO, GENERAL SECRETARY OF
THE ALLIANCE OF EVANGELICAL CHURCHES
AND MISSION ORGANIZATIONS OF CHAD

48
Get Out of Jail Free

K onan's life could not get any worse. Here he was, rotting in an Ivory Coast prison, for a murder he did not commit.

Though the police suspected Konan was guilty, they could not assemble enough evidence to convict him. So to keep him from getting out of jail while they were still gathering evidence against him, they repeatedly asked the judge to postpone his trial.

Like most of the prison's 4,000 inmates, Konan was a Muslim and regularly went to pray at the prison mosque. Day after day he asked Allah for one thing: a trial. Konan was certain that in a court of law he would be proved innocent.

But days dragged on into weeks, weeks into months, and months into years. After six years, Konan began to lose faith in Allah. One day he decided to visit the Christian chapel in the prison. The pastor noticed him as he entered and took a seat in the rear. After the service was over, Konan slipped out before anyone could speak to him.

But the next week he came back, and this time he sat a little closer to the front. When the pastor gave an opportunity for prayer requests, Konan stood up.

"Please ask your God to help me get a trial date!" Konan pleaded.

As the pastor prayed for him, Konan thought to himself, *"There's something different about this man's prayer!"* He could sense this man's conviction that his prayer was being heard.

The next week Konan entered the chapel grinning from ear to ear. "I'm getting out, Pastor!" he said excitedly. "I was called for trial this week, and they acquitted me! For six long years I prayed to Allah, but he never answered me. You asked your Jesus one time, and within a week I'm going home! I have no doubt that Jesus is real, and I want Him to be my God!"

After Konan got out of prison, he began regularly attending the pastor's church. And today he, too, serves the Lord in prison ministry!

ദ്ധ

"O you who hear prayer, to you all men will come."

PSALM 65:2

Lord, teach me to pray with greater faith, confident that You really do hear my prayers.

49
Never in Vain

The Lord can use anyone and anything—even a stubborn cow—to reach the lost with the gospel.

The Saura tribals of eastern India were doubly cut off from the rest of the world: first by a mountain barrier, and second by their intense fear of evil spirits which they believed controlled their lives. Deeply suspicious of outsiders, the Sauras appeared to be unreachable as far as the gospel was concerned.

But in 1970 the Lord called one man, Narayan Paul, to leave his well-paying job in order to bring the message of salvation to the Sauras. For many years he toiled among them, trying to communicate the gospel to them in any way he could think of. But after eleven years of preaching, not even one Saura had turned to the Lord. Though he was often tempted to give up, the call of his Master compelled him to press on.

One day while sitting under a tree, he noticed a small boy trying to move a lazy cow. He pushed and pulled, but the stubborn animal would not budge. Determined to succeed, the boy then tied a rope around her calf's neck and began leading it away. Sure enough, the mother cow followed directly behind. The Lord then spoke to Narayan's heart: *"If you want to reach the Saura people, first win the children. Then their parents will follow."*

With new inspiration, Narayan returned to the Saura villages. He began telling stories to the children and teaching them songs about

155

Jesus. Before long, the Lord had won their hearts. In a short time their parents also followed. After eleven years of faithful sowing, Narayan finally began to reap a harvest of souls.

In 1981 one Saura family came to the Lord. The next year 20 more believed, and Narayan organized the first Saura church. Today there are over 35 churches among the Sauras, together numbering more than 4,000 believers. Challenged by Narayan's example, the Sauras have become missionaries themselves, going out to evangelize and plant churches in other villages.

Often we pray and witness to family, friends, and neighbors, seemingly to no avail. But whenever we feel the slightest bit of discouragement, let us remember the persistence of Narayan Paul. Truly, our labors for the Lord are never in vain.

෬෬

"Let us not become weary in doing good, for at the proper time we will reap a harvest if we do not give up."

GALATIANS 6:9

Lord, let me not be weary in sharing the gospel, even when I do not see fruit.

ADI NARAYAN PAUL, FOUNDER-DIRECTOR OF
NEW LIFE ASSOCIATION, INDIA

50
Not Without Witness

INDIA

After much personal reflection, young Savara concluded that somewhere in the world, there must be a better god than the hill gods he knew and feared. But how would he find out about Him?

A member of the Saura tribe, Savara was taught growing up that the evil spirits living in the hills always had to be appeased through animal sacrifices. Because the Sauras lived in fear of the hill gods, they had to regularly slaughter their livestock as offerings to the gods—even though they were wretchedly poor.

Savara could not understand how the hill gods could expect so many animal sacrifices from them. Didn't the gods realize that his people were sick and dying from hunger because they had to devote most of their meager resources to these sacrifices? He began imagining that somewhere in the universe there must be a God who loved and cared for the poor, instead of burdening them with costly sacrifices and then silently sitting and watching them suffer.

Before long, an evangelist came to Savara's village announcing the good news of Jesus Christ. He spoke of a God who loved people and went to great trouble to save them from their problems. As the preacher continued to share, Savara realized that this was the God he'd been searching for all along.

Savara gladly received Jesus as his Lord and Savior and was baptized. Today he pastors a church in a Saura village while also leading missionary efforts to bring the gospel to nearby villages.

Some Christians today wonder about the fate of those who die without ever having heard the gospel. While the Bible clearly states that those who have not heard will not be saved simply because of their ignorance, it does teach that whoever truly seeks the Lord will find Him—including people like Savara who live in the uttermost ends of the earth.

CБCЯ

"You will seek me and find me when you seek me with all your heart."

JEREMIAH 29:13

Lord, the world is still full of people who don't know You, who are seeking to fill the void in their hearts. Please reveal Yourself to them.

51
Only One Chance

MYANMAR (BURMA)

F or twenty-five years he had fiercely resisted anything to do with Christianity. But with his life crumbling into pieces around him, he thought, "Should I give this foreign god a chance to prove himself?"

Like many of his fellow Buddhist countrymen, Kein Maung Thein hated Christianity because of it association with British colonialism. How could any Burmese in his right mind bow to the God of the British, after seeing how they had oppressed them and completely plundered their land? Filled with indignation, Kein even married a nominal Christian woman, hoping to convert her to Buddhism.

After his marriage Kein embarked on a personal quest for God. For fourteen years he devoted himself to probing the mysteries of Buddhism. During that time he also taught Buddhist doctrine to novice monks.

But after fourteen years of intense study, Kein finally had to admit that Buddhism could not show him the path to God. The Buddha himself had taught that each person had to find his own path, and after fourteen years Kein was no closer to finding it than when he had first begun.

Discouraged, Kein drifted aimlessly for another eleven years. He became an alcoholic and his life began to fall apart. Finally, on the verge of despair, he decided to give a chance to the Christian God whom he had hated for twenty-five years. "If you are really God," he cried out, "then deliver me from the curse of alcohol!"

To Kein's astonishment, his craving for alcohol entirely disappeared! Realizing that Jesus Christ had rescued him where Buddha had failed him, he received Jesus as his Savior and Lord. His soul was filled with a peace and a joy he had never known. At last he had found the path to God!

Burdened to show this same path to other searching Buddhists, Kein founded Bethany Evangelical Mission in 1985. The man who used to indoctrinate Buddhist monks now devotes his days to sharing the gospel with them. His greatest desire is to see all the Buddhist monasteries in Burma transformed into Bible schools.

Kein gave Jesus Christ a chance, and the Lord did not fail him. Do you know someone whom you can also encourage to give Jesus a chance?

CRCR

"Taste and see that the Lord is good; blessed is the man who takes refuge in him."

PSALM 34:8

Lord, all who have truly tasted You and tried You have never been disappointed. Hallelujah!

KEIN MAUNG THEIN, FOUNDER-DIRECTOR OF
BETHANY EVANGELICAL MINISTRY, MYANMAR,
WITH HIS WIFE YIN YIN MYINT

52
Double Blessing

Soejitno could not believe his eyes. Again he re-read the same verse in the Koran. Was it really true?

Soejitno had been diligently reading the Koran since his youth. He must have read this particular verse many times before without giving it a second thought, but this time it seemed to leap off the page: *"Isa (the Muslim name for Jesus), the son of Mary, will become a prominent judge."*

It was right there in front of him. Jesus, the founder of Christianity, would be God's appointed judge! And his own scripture, the Koran, stated this!

Soejitno was frightened. How could he stand before Jesus in judgment, not knowing what this man expected from him? The only information he knew about Jesus was the little the Koran mentioned about him. From that day on, he began seeking more information about his future Judge. Often he would wake up during the night and cry out to God to show him the truth.

God answered his prayer by sending a Christian woman across his path. She gave him a Bible and explained to him who Isa, the son of Mary, was.

"The Koran is right," she said, confirming what Soejitno had read earlier. "Jesus will judge the world one day. Why don't you meet Him now as your Savior instead of waiting to meet him on Judgment Day?"

In the days that followed, two wonderful things happened. First, Soejitno fell in love with Jesus Christ and asked Him to be his Savior. Second, he also fell in love with this Christian woman and asked her to be his wife! Overjoyed at this double blessing in his life, he decided to get baptized and married on the same day: December 8, 1968. Soejitno continued to grow in the Lord, aided by his loving wife. After retiring from the police force, he started a radio ministry which broadcasts the gospel throughout Indonesia, bringing God's Word inside millions of Muslim homes.

Soejitno went home to be with the Lord in September 1998. And on that day when he stands before Jesus, the Great Judge, he will be so thankful that he knew him as Lord and Savior. Do you have the same confidence?

CSCR

S.A. SOEJITNO, FOUNDER OF
BATU RADIO MINISTRY, INDONESIA

"For we must all appear before the judgment seat of Christ."

2 CORINTHIANS 5:10

Lord, let my faith in You never waver, that I may be kept safe until the last day.

53
The Sign of the Cross

IRAN

He was eighty-five years old, but still he had not found the answers to his questions. Where could he turn to find the truth before he died?

A Muslim all his life in a small Iranian village, Parviz knew in his heart that eight and a half decades of Islamic teaching had not given him peace. As he drew nearer to his final hour, he became increasingly discouraged and desperate for answers.

One day he cried out to God to reveal the truth to him. When he lifted his eyes up to the sky, he suddenly saw a radiant light in the shape of a cross hovering over his village. Believing this to be the answer to his prayer, Parviz dropped to his knees and exclaimed, "Lord of the cross, I believe in You!"

Parviz did not know anything about the Lord of the cross, except that He was worshipped in churches. Because the government had shut down all the churches in his area, he decided to travel 600 miles to Tehran, the capital city, where he thought he would be able to find at least one church.

Upon arrival he did manage to locate a church. As he walked up to the entrance, the ushers—seeing his appearance and assuming that he was a Muslim who had mistakenly come to the wrong building—pointed him towards the mosque across the street. Parviz firmly replied, "No, I have come seeking a church," and proceeded to share his testimony to the ushers. Once a month he makes the

600-mile trek from his village to Tehran to attend church, so he can grow in his Christian faith.

The Lord will always reveal Himself to those who cry out for wisdom and understanding. Are you seeking Him now?

കൃ൩

"If you call out for insight and cry aloud for understanding, and if you look for it as for silver and search for it as for hidden treasure, then you will understand the fear of the Lord and find the knowledge of God."

PROVERBS 2:3-5

Lord, please give me the same hunger and thirst for Your wisdom and understanding.

54
Nothing Will Harm You

BENIN (WEST AFRICA)

As they heard the voodoo priests summoning the evil spirits to strike them dead, Gregore and his family trembled. Would Jesus be able to deliver them from this?

Only two months ago in their village of Ouedo, Gregore and one of his wives had become Christians. A month later his other wife, who was a voodoo priestess, also decided to become a Christian. Little did they know that in just a few weeks they would be facing a massive challenge to their new faith.

One evening the village chief sent messengers to Gregore's house bearing his staff, a voodoo fetish. They asked him to follow the staff to the chief's home. But Gregore refused, saying that because he had become a Christian, he would no longer follow the voodoo staff anywhere.

When the chief heard that Gregore had refused his summons—an act of bold defiance that no one else had ever dared to do—he was furious. He immediately ordered the village priests to start the "Man Afokou," a seven-day voodoo ceremony to call up the evil spirits to strike them dead.

Having formerly been a voodoo priestess herself, Gregore's wife knew the power of the Man Afokou. So for seven days Gregore and his wives cried out to the Lord to deliver them from the powers of darkness. At the end of the week, all of them were still alive and well.

Greatly embarrassed, the village leaders then decided to finish off Gregore and his wives by another method. A few days later they hired thugs to kidnap one of his wives while she was gathering firewood in the forest. Fortunately, some local women heard her scream and ran back to the village to call Gregore. When he arrived at the scene, the thugs beat him up and stabbed him with a knife. But after some negotiating they agreed to release her, and Gregore went to the hospital for medical treatment.

Terribly frustrated that Gregore and his wives were still alive, the chief called together all the priests to perform the most dangerous voodoo ceremony of all. With the whole village gathered and watching, the head priest slaughtered different animals on the altar and began calling down terrible curses upon the three Christians. Everyone expected that before long, they would surely fall over dead.

But suddenly before their very eyes, the voodoo priest himself fell dead over the sacrifice! Everyone fled, terrified. The following Sunday, the believers held a special time of praise and worship to the Lord. Other pagan villagers also came, curious to know more about the God who had defied the voodoo powers. Since that time, there has been no more opposition to the gospel in Ouedo, and even the voodoo priests have come to church begging for the power that only Jesus can give.

"I have given you authority to trample on snakes and scorpions and to overcome all the power of the enemy; nothing will harm you."

LUKE 10:19

Lord, thank you for Your promise to always protect me from the powers of darkness when I call out to You.

55
Showers of Blessing

The rain was coming down in buckets, right through the make-shift tent roof made of palm leaves and onto the heads of thousands of delegates. The Lord was not answering their prayers for good weather, and it seemed like all their conference planning was turning out to be a complete washout. Should they just cancel and send everyone back home?

For months, the Saura tribal Christians had been looking forward to their annual church convention. Members from 35 Saura churches would be coming down from their remote hill villages for three exciting days of worship, preaching, and fellowship. In preparation, the organizers had converted a large paddy field into a makeshift campground. In the center they had constructed a huge convention tent out of branches and palm leaves, and on the periphery they had erected numerous smaller tents to shelter the delegates.

By the time the main speaker arrived, three to four thousand delegates had already gathered. The conference was all set to begin, when suddenly it started pouring rain. Within a few minutes, the organizers realized that the palm leaf tent roof—intended only to provide shade from the sun—could not keep out the falling rain. Before long everyone was completely soaked.

What to do? The organizers decided to wait out the downpour. For several hours they watched glumly as the campground slowly turned into a shallow pool. Discouraged, they cancelled all the services for that day and instructed the people to pray. Unless the skies cleared up by the following day, they would have to cancel the rest of the convention.

The next morning it was still raining. Completely disheartened, the organizers wondered what had gone wrong. Was the Lord withholding His blessing from this meeting? Did they fail to pray hard enough?

They were about to cancel the rest of the convention when a group of Saura church elders came forward. "Our church members don't want you to cancel," they pleaded. "If we go back now, the other villagers will mock us. They will surely ask, 'If your God is as powerful as you say He is, then why couldn't He stop the rain?' We have already come all this way, so we don't mind even if we have to listen in the rain!"

Upon seeing their commitment, the main speaker was moved. "If they are willing to listen in the rain, then I am also willing to preach in the rain!"

So the crowd began to happily listen to God's Word in the rain. By afternoon, the rain had stopped. The Lord greatly blessed the remainder of the convention: around 100 people gave their hearts to Jesus Christ, 260 were baptized, and thousands left with strengthened hearts.

How often do we plan an event—whether a small evangelistic gathering or a large meeting—and decide to cancel it when things fail to go according to our original human plans: low turnout, bad weather, etc.? Or how often do we plan to attend a meeting—whether a church service or a special conference—and decide at the last minute not to go because of busy-ness, laziness, or bad weather? We would do well to remember the example of the Saura believers, whose commitment to go ahead with the Lord's meetings despite great personal inconvenience yielded true showers of blessing for them.

"Let us not give up meeting together, as some are in the habit of doing, but let us encourage one another—and all the more as you see the Day approaching."

HEBREWS 10:25

Lord, help me to learn from the Saura's commitment to Your meetings.

56
No Idol Speech

Ten-year-old David tensed at his teacher's words.

"I want each of you to bring some money to class next time so we can all celebrate the Saraswati festival together!"

Every year in India during the Hindu festival celebrating Saraswati, the goddess of education, children bring money to school to help pay for the celebration. David clearly knew that participating in idol festivals was wrong, but how could he stand up to his teacher? He had been taught never to talk back to elders. Besides, he was always soft-spoken and gentle.

Suddenly David blurted out, "I can't bring in money. I'm a Christian!"

Slightly irritated, his teacher answered, "That makes no difference. Saraswati is for everyone, whether you are Hindu or Christian. Just because you're a Christian doesn't mean you can't celebrate the Saraswati festival."

"But my god is not the same as your god," countered little David, suddenly growing bold. "Your god is made of clay," he said, pointing to the idol next to his teacher. "If I push it, it will fall over. But you cannot push over my God because He is a living God! If I call upon your god for help, it will not get up and help me. But my God can help me in all things!"

The teacher became annoyed at this outburst from such a young child. And before he could respond any further, David grabbed the idol with both hands, tipped it to one side, and then brought it back upright.

"See?" he said triumphantly. "Your god is a helpless god, but my God is a living God!"

The teacher was speechless, while the other children laughed that their teacher had been silenced by quiet little David!

CԾCԾ

"Do you hear what these children are saying?" they asked him. "Yes," replied Jesus, "have you never read, 'From the lips of children and infants you have ordained praise'?"

MATTHEW 21:16

Lord, please give me the courage and faith to speak up for You every day.

57
Suffering Without Shame

INDIA

The phone was ringing at 11:00 p.m., so Lourdes knew it had to be an emergency. After picking up the receiver, all she could hear at first was a quiet sob.

"It's me, Surang," came a low voice finally. "Papa found out that Somsak and I had become Christians! The family got suspicious because we hadn't done our offerings at the family altar for a long time. Today the whole family came together, and Papa got very angry when we confessed that we had become Christians. He tried to force us to burn incense on the spot! We refused, so he began to beat us. Now he wants to throw us out of the house! O, what shall we do?"

Lourdes had only a few seconds to think before answering. In Thailand, only rebellious children were thrown out of the house, which meant that the two siblings were about to lose their good reputations.

"Don't leave your house, Surang," Lourdes advised. "Has Jesus failed you yet? Has He not been good to you all these months since you gave your life to Him?"

"Yes, He's been very good to me," sobbed Surang. "I know He cares for me."

"Then don't you consider it worthwhile to suffer for Him? He suffered so much more for you!"

After putting down the receiver, Lourdes stared into the midnight darkness. She knew this day would come, but she did not expect it would come this soon. She recalled the first day they met, when Surang and her brother Somsak signed up for her free English class on the condition that they stay for a one-hour Bible study afterwards. Coming from a Buddhist family, they initially did not like the Bible study. But as the Word of God began to sink into their hearts, they gradually became convicted of their sin and their need for a Savior. One year later, both of them decided to accept Jesus as their Savior and Lord.

After becoming Christians, Surang and Somsak were so eager to grow in their faith that they started attending Sunday services and prayer meetings as well as taking on new responsibilities at church. They also quietly stopped offering incense and food at the family altar.

But now their conversion was no longer a secret, because Papa had found out. Lourdes knew that only the Lord could give them strength during this crisis, so she prayed fervently to the Lord to help them.

The next morning, Somsak came to visit Lourdes. She immediately saw that his father's flat wooden stick had left many marks on him. But he brought good news: one of his older brothers had persuaded Papa not to send the two of them away. Lourdes immediately thanked the Lord for answering her prayers.

Later when she met Surang, she heard even better news. That night Surang's sister Saeng, who had seen everything that had happened, asked Surang why she and Somsak had refused to offer incense. With tears still fresh in her eyes, Surang explained to her sister who Jesus was and what He had done for her. At two o' clock in the morning, Saeng also decided to become a Christian!

Let us always remember that those who suffer for the Lord will never be put to shame.

ଔଓ

"For it has been granted to you on behalf of Christ not only to believe on him, but also to suffer for him."

PHILIPPIANS 1:29

Lord, let me never be afraid to stand up or suffer for You.

58
No Bowing Down

Should they bow down or not bow down? Should they follow their family's Buddhist customs or should they break with tradition at the cost of publicly showing disrespect to their family? The three new believers were torn with confusion.

Their grandmother had just died. Siblings Surang, Somsak, and Saeng knew that all their relatives would soon be gathering for the funeral ceremony at the Buddhist temple. At the sound of the bell, everyone would have to bow down to show respect to the spirits of their dead ancestors.

Having accepted the Lord only recently, the trio had not yet gone public (outside their immediate family) with their faith. If they refused to bow down at the funeral, then everyone would immediately know that they were deliberately rejecting their family's Buddhist heritage—and they could only imagine what the consequences would be. Would they be able to withstand the pressure?

Seeking counsel, the three siblings telephoned the local evangelist, Lourdes, and shared their dilemma with her. After listening to them Lourdes answered, "I'll come to the funeral along with some other Christians, and we'll pray for you in the background. Just trust the Lord to give you strength to stand firm for what you believe!"

On the day of the funeral, nearly 200 people gathered in the temple. The air was heavy with incense. The Buddhist monk performed the funeral rites in front of the large Buddha statue. At the sound of the bell, everyone bowed down—everyone except Surang, Somsak, and Saeng. Praying the whole time for strength, they bravely remained standing until the end of the ceremony.

A murmur went through the crowd. "Those three recently became Christians! That is why they did not bow. Where did they get that courage?"

Like Shadrach, Meshach, and Abednego, these three boldly stood alone against the tide of intense social pressure. And like their Biblical forebears, they also earned respect for their courage to stand up for what they believed was true.

Do you have the same courage?

०३०३

"We want you to know, O king, that we will not serve your gods or worship the image of gold you have set up."

DANIEL 3:18

Lord, is my life a courageous witness for You? Help me to live in such a way that no one would doubt my total commitment to you.

59
Faith Comes From Overhearing

Suwandi's sister had invited some of her friends over to their village home. He could hear them reading and discussing something from a book, but they were whispering as if afraid of being overheard. Curious, he tried to listen in on their conversation, but he could not make sense of it.

That night after his sister had gone to sleep, Suwandi opened her schoolbag and found a book with the words "Jesus Christ" written on the cover. It was a Christian book! He flipped through a few pages to confirm that it was so. How could she read such offensive material? It was his duty as her brother to scold her, so she would not go down the wrong path.

The next day he lectured her sternly: "I read that book in your schoolbag, and I'm warning you: don't read it! We're Muslims, remember?"

But his sister's friends came again. This time they used pictures on a wooden board to explain the fire of hell and the Last Judgment. Suwandi pretended not to notice; but because the subject was so interesting, he watched carefully from a distance and tried his best to overhear their conversation.

After they finished their discussion, one of the Christian friends came over to Suwandi and invited him to join their next meeting.

Caught off guard, he pretended to be annoyed and gave them a non-committal response. But that night he lay in bed tossing and turning, wondering why he was so opposed to Christianity. Did he simply hate it without reason? If so, then shouldn't he at least be open to learning more about it?

From that time onward, Suwandi began to cautiously explore Christianity. He started reading some Christian books, and his sister's friends kept coming to their home to explain the Bible to them. As the days went by, he grew more and more interested in what they were saying. Finally, on the day that he memorized John 3:16, the Lord convicted him of his sin and his need for salvation. He asked the Lord to forgive him and received Jesus Christ as his Savior.

Suwandi came to know the Lord through overhearing the gospel from someone else. Have you recently given someone a chance to hear the same gospel from your lips?

☙❧

"Consequently, faith comes from hearing the message, and the message is heard through the word of Christ."

ROMANS 10:17

Lord, please take my lips and let them be filled with messages from Thee.

60
A Widow's Might

E verything was going well for Rodel and Jocelyn until the monsoon rains hit their island. Soon their entire village was flooded; and to their dismay, the waters swept over their backyard well, contaminating it with fresh mud.

After the rains stopped, Rodel went outside, climbed down into the well, and began hauling out the accumulated mud. He was slightly feverish, and his body ached from the backbreaking labor, but he knew he could not stop until the well was thoroughly cleaned out. At last he finished the task and collapsed into bed.

Rodel never recovered from his fever. In a few days he was diagnosed with pneumonia, and not even the doctor could reduce his high temperature. Within a few days he was dead, leaving behind a wife and two young children.

Jocelyn was devastated. What was she supposed to do now? Only a few years ago both she and her husband had come to this village to start a church. Before long the Lord had blessed them with a thriving group of new believers. They constructed a little church building and started a small Christian school, and together they dreamed of transforming their entire village with the gospel and planting more churches in nearby villages. But now, with Rodel's death, that dream seemed over.

But Jocelyn realized that in spite of her grief, she could not quit. She knew that the Lord's work had to keep on moving ahead.

Therefore she requested a minister from a nearby town to come and preach in their church on Sunday mornings. Meanwhile, she resolved to keep up with house visitation, evangelism, and discipling the new believers, besides running the small Christian school.

"Of course I miss my husband," says Jocelyn, fresh tears flooding her eyes. "But I press on, drawing strength from knowing that one day I will see him again in the presence of the Lord."

No hardship or difficulty—not even the death of her husband—could stop this widow from obeying the voice of her Master. Is there anything stopping you from obeying Him?

கஇ

JOCELYN DELADA, TEACHER AND CHURCH WORKER, PHILIPPINES, WITH HER CHILDREN JIRAH FIATH AND JAY RUE

"Forgetting what is behind and straining toward what is ahead, I press on toward the goal to win the prize for which God has called me heavenward in Christ Jesus."

PHILIPPIANS 3:13-14

Lord, in spite of the difficulties and hardships in my life, let me never cease to fully serve You.

61
The Right Workers

T he very thought of sending single ladies into the remote Shapra jungle seemed unthinkable. The Shapras were a savage warrior tribe who shrank the heads of their captives. To send in women alone there would certainly spell disaster.

Nevertheless, Rita and Sonia felt called to bring the gospel to this unreached tribe. Their mission's typical policy was to send either pairs of single men or married couples for pioneer work among unreached tribes. But seeing Rita and Sonia's determination, the mission leaders finally agreed to commission them to go there and prayed for the Lord's protection upon them.

Rita and Sonia lived in the Shapra community, working hard to learn their language. On several occasions when the Shapra men were drunk, they had to flee into the jungle to avoid their vulgar advances. Finally, after many days, the Shapra chief decided to put his faith in Jesus Christ. He began witnessing to his own tribe, and eventually a church was established there.

One day Rita and Sonia told the Shapras how their mission had been initially reluctant to send them, preferring instead to send either a pair of single men or a married couple. The Shapras then explained to them that if two single men had come, the tribe would have been threatened and would have surely killed them. If a married couple had come, the Shapra men would have killed the husband in order to have his wife. Thus, the only ones who were able to live among the Shapras and share the gospel with them were single women!

Indeed, Jesus is the Lord of the harvest and knows exactly which laborers to send into which harvest fields.

⊂8⊃

"Ask the Lord of the harvest, therefore, to send out workers into his harvest field."

MATTHEW 9:38

Lord, there are still many fields without laborers. Please send the right workers into those places, so that the final harvest may be gathered.

62
Justified by Faith

MOROCCO

Following is the stirring testimony of Ahmed Khan, who presently leads a ministry to North African Muslims.

"I was born into a family descended from the prophet Mohammed, so I grew up in a very religious home. In keeping with tradition, I began to study Islam from early childhood at a Koranic school where the Koran was memorized by heart.

"In 1953 I was awarded the title 'Fegih,' which means 'legal expert'—it is a degree given exclusively to men who memorize the entire Koran. In keeping with tradition, I began to give Koranic lessons, as boys typically start learning the Koran from age four. I taught like this for six years, and in our neighborhood mosque I was the one who would lead the prayers.

"One morning I was meditating on the Koran when I came across the following verse: *I cannot justify my soul, for the soul is deceitful*' (said by the Prophet Joseph, son of Jacob). I read this verse over and over again and became perplexed. If Joseph, a prophet, had no assurance of his own righteousness before God, then how could I or anyone else be assured of our own righteousness? I found other verses that presented the same dilemma, and I could not find any solution.

"Later I began to think, *If I am not sure of this path, then how can I teach it to others?*' Because of these doubts, I stopped teaching the Koran and entered the world of business.

"I shared my problems with a Muslim friend, who gave me the address of a center for Bible correspondence courses. Through this center I got to know a British man, with whom I began to read the New Testament.

"One day we were studying the third chapter of the Gospel of John, when I read the following verse: *'No one has ever gone into heaven except the one who came from heaven—the Son of Man'* (John 3:13). Then I understood that Jesus was not only a prophet but he was also Lord of all.

"That night while I was asleep, the Lord gave me a confirmation. I felt something like a hand touching me and a voice that said, *'Get up and read 2 Corinthians 5:18-19.'* I read it: *'All this is from God, who reconciled us to himself through Christ...'*"

In 1962 Ahmed Khan accepted the life-changing truth that no one but Jesus Christ can justify the souls of sinners. Today he strives to bring this same truth to other Muslims in his region.

ೲೞ

"Therefore, since we have been justified through faith, we have peace with God through our Lord Jesus Christ."

ROMANS 5:1

Lord, thank you for justifying my sinful heart and giving my soul rest. May You help me to share this life-transforming gospel with others.

63
A Blessed Curse

Milaz was completely fed up. Tasleem was taking every opportunity he could to ridicule him for his Christian faith. Using the most vulgar language, he would constantly curse him for having converted and accuse him of being a disgrace to his family. Stung by these attacks, Milaz often prayed, *"Lord, why can't You make him leave me alone?"*

Although Milaz tried to ignore Tasleem's words, over the months the layered hurts began to fester inside. His indifference slowly changed into anger, and he started thinking hateful thoughts against Tasleem.

One day during his prayer time, the Lord spoke to Milaz: *"Look at yourself: you're actually a worse sinner than Tasleem! He doesn't know Me, but you do—yet you don't obey Me! My Word says to bless those who curse you and pray for those who mistreat you, but the only thought you have is how to get rid of him!"*

Convicted of his sin, Milaz asked the Lord to forgive him. From that day onward whenever Tasleem cursed him, Milaz would bless him back with loving words. Irritated that his curses were having precisely the opposite effect of what he was intended, Tasleem would get even angrier and would curse him back with even harsher language. But the more Tasleem cursed him, the more Milaz blessed him. Once Tasleem blasted out, "Look at this dumb sheep! I curse him and he blesses me!" Milaz answered with a grin, "I'm glad you didn't call me a goat, because the goats will be asked to go to the left side of the Lord. I'm so glad you called me a sheep!"

Finally, Tasleem got so angry at Milaz's loving responses that he took out a knife and jabbed him. Milaz was surprised to feel no pain at all, and at that moment he knew that the Lord had given him special grace to endure his enemy's blows. In fact, his heart was filled with joy because he had been found worthy to follow in the steps of his Savior, who had also blessed His enemies while they were attacking Him. On seeing Milaz's joyful response upon being attacked, Tasleem decided to never bother him again.

Milaz's testimony challenges us to ask ourselves two questions: (1) do we need God's help to release any bitterness we may be carrying against anyone, and (2) are we doing good to those who hate us and blessing those who curse us?

ᘒᘒ

"Love your enemies, do good to those who hate you, bless those who curse you, pray for those who mistreat you."

LUKE 6:27-28

Lord, give me grace to do good to those who hate me and to bless those who curse me.

64
A Letter to God

D esperate for answers to his questions, Rockeybell wrote a letter to God, addressed it to *The Almighty God, P.O. Box Heaven, City Heaven, Country Heaven*, and mailed it. He then wondered, *"When will God answer me back?"*

Rockeybell Adatura grew up in a Muslim community. He was warned by his elders not to touch the Bible, lest the evil spirits which led Christians astray would also take over his mind.

A top-notch boxer, by the age of 16 Rockeybell had gained fame as Ghana's national flyweight boxing champion. His athletic career took him to many different places, where he always saw injustice and suffering. Increasingly confused by the apparent silence of God in the midst of such suffering, he decided to write a letter to God full of his questions. With all sincerity he mailed it and waited for a response. "God knows my heart's intent, and surely He will respond to me in some way," he thought confidently.

But as the days passed and no answer came, Rockeybell began to doubt whether or not God really existed. So at age 19 he decided to forget about religion and just enjoy life to the fullest. He indulged himself in drugs, alcohol, and women, thinking that these would give him maximum satisfaction in life. But after three years of wild living, he realized that his soul was emptier and lonelier than it had ever been.

Miserable and tired of life, Rockeybell decided to commit suicide by taking an overdose of drugs and alcohol. But it proved to be a failed suicide attempt. When he regained consciousness, he heard a still small voice calling out to him: *"You've tried everything and it has failed you. Why don't you try the Bible?"*

At first he thought he was still in a drug-induced stupor, but the strange voice repeated the same message three times. Desperate for help but afraid to touch the Bible, he wanted to know whether or not God was really speaking to him. He knelt down and prayed, *"God, if it is really You speaking, then come quickly to save me!"*

Immediately Rockeybell felt the Lord's presence flowing through his entire being. At that moment he knew that it was truly God who was talking to him! He got up and searched for a Bible. But still uncomfortable with the thought of embracing the Bible and rejecting the Koran, he placed the two books side by side and asked God to show him which one was true.

Rockeybell then began a meticulous comparison of these two books, verse by verse, cover to cover. It took him four years to complete his study. At the end of his quest, not only did he find that the Bible satisfactorily answered all of his former questions, but he also put his faith in Jesus Christ.

Today Rockeybell is a noted Bible teacher, evangelistic author, and Christian scholar in Ghana.

"Your word is a lamp to my feet and a light for my path."

PSALM 119:105

Lord, please give me a greater desire to saturate myself in Your Word, that it might completely transform my heart.

ROCKYBELL ADATURA, FOUNDER-DIRECTOR OF
ADATURA RESEARCH PUBLICATIONS, GHANA

65
The Right Button

P.G. Vargis suddenly faced a dilemma while walking down the street to a church meeting. He noticed that his shirt was missing a button.

What should he do? It was the only shirt he had with him—an old faded blue shirt. As a traveling preacher, he lived off whatever was given to him by the churches. But this time, he didn't even have ten cents in his pocket to buy a new button.

How embarrassing it would be to walk into the next church meeting looking so shabby! Moreover, the next day he was scheduled to preach at another church. The thought of going as the Lord's servant in such an undignified manner greatly concerned him.

With child-like faith P.G. began to pray, asking the Lord for either a button or ten cents to buy a new one. Then he realized that his other buttons were old and faded. *"Lord,"* he prayed again, *"one new button with four old buttons would look so awkward. So please either give me an old blue button or fifty cents to buy five new ones."*

He had scarcely finished praying when his eyes were drawn to something lying on the ground. Right there in front of him was an old blue button! He picked it up and compared it to his other shirt buttons. It matched the other four perfectly! With a prayer of thanksgiving he sewed it on and continued on his way to the meeting place.

Do we really believe that the Lord will take care of our needs, even down to the last button?

ය CR

"Do not be anxious about anything, but in everything, by prayer and petition, with thanksgiving, present your requests to God."

PHILIPPIANS 4:6

Thank you, Lord, for caring about even the smallest need in my life.

66
In His Time

INDIA

H er father and mother had died. Her brothers had scattered. What would become of the little orphan girl?

The only daughter of wealthy Nepali Buddhist parents, Angela was living peacefully with her family until a series of bitter tragedies ripped apart her life. First, criminals ambushed her father's vehicle and hacked him to death. Then her mother died of tuberculosis. Following this, her five distressed and confused brothers ran off in different directions.

In just a short time everything was gone: all the family, all the joy, and all the stability Angela had ever known. One of her older brothers took her along with him, started a small restaurant, and had her help out there as he had no resources to send her to school. But he desperately wanted his little sister to get an education, so he brought her to the home of a well-known pastor who ran a Christian school.

Angela's brother explained her plight to the pastor and pleaded with him to let his little sister work as a servant in his house in exchange for free schooling. Moved with compassion, the pastor decided to take her in—not as a servant girl, but rather as his own newly-adopted daughter!

Angela started attending school, where she received not only a good education but also solid Bible teaching. In time, the Lord opened her heart and she decided to become a Christian. After she

205

finished her schooling she told her adopted father, "Even though I am sad to have lost my earthly parents, I realize that through it all I came to know my Heavenly Father."

Angela decided to attend Bible college, and there she met her future husband. Today both of them are serving the Lord in bringing the gospel to the Nepali community in India.

Angela's story reminds us that in His time, the Lord will transform a hopeless situation into something beautiful. Are you willing to wait for His time?

ೞೞ

"He has made everything beautiful in its time."

ECCLESIASTES 3:11

Lord, help me to be patient and trust that You will make all my trials and struggles beautiful—in Your time.

67
A Father's Nightmare

BANGLADESH

"*Lord! Why must my two daughters suffer beatings on account of me?*"

Before Toffazal and his wife became Christians, they had already given two of their daughters in marriage to Muslim men. And in keeping with the joint family system practiced throughout South Asia, their two daughters moved into their in-laws' homes after marriage, as sons typically stay with their parents even after marriage.

But when the in-laws found out that Toffazal and his wife had converted to Christianity, they were shocked. How could the parents of their daughters-in-law stoop so low? For both of these Muslim families, it was shameful to be related—even through marriage—to anyone who had turned their backs on Allah. As a result, they began to mentally and physically persecute Toffazal's two daughters.

When Toffazal heard this news, he was devastated. He cried out to the Lord day and night on behalf of his two precious daughters, whose tear-streaked faces he could not see but whose pain he felt as if it was his own body being beaten. It seemed so unfair: why should his Muslim daughters suffer, when it was he and his wife who had become Christians?

In spite of all this, Toffazal did not waver in his faith but instead continued to witness all the more boldly for the Lord in his village. In time, the Lord honored his faithfulness with a double blessing. First, the in-laws eventually stopped persecuting his daughters. And second, through his testimony several villagers put their trust in the Lord.

Toffazal learned early on in his Christian walk that the Lord sometimes allows His children to go through difficult and seemingly unfair trials. He also learned that if we remain faithful to him during these times, then we will shine like stars in the night sky and earn great rewards, both in this life and in the life to come.

$$\text{ЖЖ}$$

"So then, those who suffer according to God's will should commit themselves to their faithful Creator and continue to do good."

1 PETER 4:19

Lord, please give me grace to go through all my trials without doubting Your goodness or justice.

68
Romeo Repents

THAILAND

With an impish smile and a mischievous gleam in his eyes, Tu quietly congratulated himself. He had just figured out how to hook his next date!

Ever since his teenage years, Tu had been smoking and drinking. But his specialty was womanizing: strong and good-looking, he prided himself in being able to woo and win the hearts of beautiful Thai girls.

One day he saw a new pretty face, and immediately he began to plan how he could connect with her. He discovered to his glee that she had accidentally left her notebook in a friend's place. Grabbing the notebook, he returned home with a sly grin on his face and relished the thought of enjoying her company soon.

Tu called up the young lady, introduced himself, and offered to return her notebook. She politely requested him if they could meet at church the following Sunday, so she could collect it from him. Tu quickly assented: after all, what was the problem with attending church once if he could get his next date there?

After his first church visit, Tu found himself returning again and again. As the preaching of the Word of God began to convict his heart, his interest gradually shifted from the girl to the gospel. He had never heard anything like what he was hearing here, and he realized that he could not dismiss its burning truth from his soul.

A few months later, the pastor sensed that he needed to ask Tu about his spiritual condition. He called Tu aside and asked him to read Galatians 5:19-21: *"The acts of the sinful nature are obvious: sexual immorality, impurity, and debauchery; idolatry and witchcraft; hatred, discord, jealousy, fits of rage, selfish ambition, dissensions, factions and envy; drunkenness, orgies, and the like. I warn you, as I did before, that those who live like this will not inherit the kingdom of God."*

After reading these verses, Tu trembled and replied, "Pastor, I have committed every one of these acts! What should I do?"

The pastor explained that Jesus Christ had died for all of his sins; and if he put his trust in Him, then God would forgive him of everything he had ever done. Tu was so moved by the message of the gospel that he immediately decided to receive Jesus as his Lord and Savior!

After some time, Tu's Buddhist parents discovered that their son had become a Christian. They were both furious and disappointed: his mother wept and his father cursed him. In spite of their reaction, he knew he had to obey the Lord's call upon his life. Tu left home to attend Bible school and later entered Christian ministry.

Isn't God worthy of our praise, for pursuing us even when we were living in rebellion against Him?

"I was found by those who did not seek me; I revealed myself to those who did not ask for me."

ROMANS 10:20

Lord, how is it that You pursue sinners in love and extend Your grace even to the most unworthy of people? I bless Your holy name!

69
To the Rescue

The phone rang at 7:00 a.m.

"Your younger brother's heart and kidneys have failed," came the voice on the other end. "He's in very critical condition."

Within a few moments Cahya was out the door of his home in Java and on his way to the hospital on another island in the Indonesian archipelago. Weaving through traffic, he raced to the ferry. Depending on ferry lines and traffic, the trip could take as long as six hours. There was only one thing on his mind as he sped along.

"Please Lord, before Aneka dies, let me have a chance to apologize to him for the mistakes I made in the past. And please give me one more chance to convince him to believe in You."

It was noon by the time Cahya reached the hospital. Anxiously he asked for his brother's room.

"We're sorry," came the reply. "Your brother isn't here. He's been shifted to a better hospital on Java."

Cahya's heart sank. Would Aneka die before they could meet? Unbelievably, he had to turn around and take the same ferry back the way he had just come. This time, the line at the dock was two hours long. After what seemed like an eternity, he boarded the ferry, crossed the narrow strait, and disembarked on Java. Speeding and praying all the way, he finally reached the hospital.

Most people were leaving as Cahya rushed inside, as visiting hours were almost over. He finally reached his brother in Room 53. Aneka was having difficulty breathing and was in great pain, but at least he was still conscious. He recognized his older brother.

Cahya apologized to Aneka for his past mistakes and then began sharing with him about Jesus Christ, his greatest need at that hour. Whenever Cahya had shared the gospel with him in the past, Aneka had always argued back. But this time he just kept quiet and listened carefully.

"Although you have rejected Him your whole life, if you invite Him to be your Savior now He will still save you. Do you want to receive Him?"

Aneka nodded. They prayed together.

"Where is Jesus now?" Cahya asked.

Putting his right hand on his chest, Aneka answered, "In my heart."

Greatly relieved, Cahya stayed a little longer and then left the hospital. It was 7:00 p.m. Twelve hours of running to save a soul had paid off! The next morning at 5:10 a.m. the phone rang again: Aneka had just passed away. Putting down the receiver, Cahya bowed his head in grief but quietly thanked the Lord for giving him one final chance to rescue his brother from the clutches of hell.

"Be merciful to those who doubt; snatch others from the fire and save them."

JUDE 22-23

Lord, would You show me someone who needs to hear the gospel soon, before it is too late?

70
Spying Unto Salvation

CUBA

When Juan began attending church in Havana, his hearty Christian spirit was immediately evident. For weeks he never missed a service. He prayed, sang, worshipped, and ministered to others. He had a powerful testimony of his own conversion as well as a glowing letter of recommendation from his former pastor.

Despite the many government restrictions on Christianity in Cuba, Juan spoke out boldly for Christ and fearlessly against the Communist regime. "God bless you!" he would greet fellow Christians on the streets. "Praise the Lord!" he would proclaim whenever he saw his pastor.

One day after months of faithful church attendance, Juan came to the pastor's house.

"Pastor, may I speak with you privately?"

"Sure Juan, come in!"

"Pastor," Juan began hesitantly, "I am not who you think I am. I am a Secret Service agent. I've been sent by the government to report on any anti-Communist activity within your church.

"I've been an atheist all my life, and I've never experienced anything like what I'm experiencing now. Your people are good people. I am so touched by their love and concern for me. Pastor, I want to accept this Jesus that you are all so excited about!"

There in his living room, the pastor explained the gospel fully to Juan. He repented of his sins and received Jesus as his Savior.

Because Cuban Secret Service agents are under contract for life, Juan has not been able to live a typical Christian life. He cannot attend church regularly, nor can he openly read his Bible or pray. In spite of all this, Juan remains a living example of the power of the gospel to save even the most unlikely of sinners!

∞

"Yet to all who received him, to those who believed in his name, he gave the right to become children of God."

JOHN 1:12

Lord, thank you for giving all kinds of sinners—including me—the right to become Your children!

71
Faith Under Fire

IRAN

Akbar had never sat through this kind of interrogation before: three hours of non-stop fiery grilling. What answer should he give the Muslim priest?

Partially deaf and illiterate, Akbar was only eight years old when he began working as a servant in a Christian home. His masters taught him how to read and write, and they also shared the gospel with him. In time, Akbar decided to become a follower of Jesus Christ.

Akbar's father, while encouraged by his son's academic progress, was not happy at all when he learned that his son had become a Christian. So one day he told Akbar that he needed to bring him to the doctor. When they arrived at their destination, Akbar realized that his father had lied to him: the "doctor" turned out to be an imam—a Muslim priest. Then he realized what his father's intentions were.

Once inside, the imam began to interrogate Akbar. "How much money have the Christians promised you? We'll give you more. What type of wife have they promised you? We'll give you a better one." In this manner the imam continued for three hours, using every conceivable argument to persuade Akbar to give up Christianity and return to Islam. Akbar just listened quietly the whole time.

After three hours, the imam wanted to know Akbar's response. The young man just looked straight at him and replied, "Sir, you are a sinner. You need to repent and ask Jesus Christ for forgiveness!"

Akbar's father was aghast at his son's response and began to cry. The imam, trying his best to remain calm, told the father, "Don't worry. Your son's head is hot. Bring him back later!"

Once they had left the office, Akbar turned to his father and said, "You told me that you were taking me to the doctor, but instead you brought me to the imam. A religion that uses deception to persuade others cannot be true."

C3CR

"But make up your mind not to worry beforehand how you will defend yourselves. For I will give you words and wisdom that none of your adversaries will be able to resist or contradict."

LUKE 21:14-15

Lord, may I never fail to remain faithful to You, no matter how much I am attacked for my faith.

72
Better Than a University Diploma

ALGERIA

K halid knew that he had left his country and come all the way here just for his university studies. If so, was it right for him to be spending this much time on the side exploring another religion?

Khalid was born and brought up in a Muslim home in Algeria. As a teenager, he had an opportunity to visit his older brother in Europe. There, for the first time in his life, he met some Christians; and he was surprised to find that instead of being bad people, they were actually a very friendly, loving, and God-fearing group. They gave him a Bible, which he accepted. He returned back to Algeria very much challenged by their way of life, which he had not seen lived out in his own Muslim community.

Two years later, Khalid was accepted as a foreign student at a university in Sweden. When he arrived on campus, he once again met some Christians. Naturally he started thinking again about the differences between Islam and Christianity. But was it something worth pursuing, or should he just stick to his academics?

Around this time, Khalid met a former Muslim who later became a Christian. Curious to learn the reason for his conversion, Khalid struck up a friendship with him. His new friend was very open to sharing with him; and after many hours of conversation and Bible study together, Khalid also decided to become a Christian. With great joy he received Jesus as his Lord and Savior and was baptized.

Khalid was so excited about the changes in his life that he spent the next five years actively sharing his testimony with other Muslims throughout Europe. Afterwards, the Lord called him back to Algeria to be a witness in his homeland. Today Khalid pastors a church there and leads an evangelistic ministry to his fellow countrymen.

While most Western Christians will never set foot on foreign soil, particularly in countries closed to missionaries, they often don't realize that God has brought those countries' citizens right in our own neighborhoods as foreign students—most of whom have never heard the gospel. If we can make the most of these opportunities to befriend them, then we can send them back home with something far better than just a university diploma!

ೞೞ

"As for the foreigner who does not belong to your people Israel but has come from a distant land because of your name—for men will hear of your great name... when he comes... then hear from heaven, your dwelling place, and do whatever the foreigner asks of you, so that all the peoples of the earth may know your name and fear you."

I KINGS 8:41-43

Lord, are there any foreign students or professionals in my area to whom You want me to reach out?

73
Understanding the Mystery

UGANDA

Alone and dying on a banana plantation in the jungle, Alex's life seemed to be quickly coming to a bitter end.

When Alex Mitala Mukasa was just a baby, his drunkard father abandoned the family and left his mother alone to raise their eleven children. Unable to afford a proper education, Alex had to drop out of school in the seventh grade. At age 15 he moved to Kampala, the capital city, where his ruthless spirit and skill at drug dealing soon led him to become a gang leader.

Two years later, he was a wanted criminal. Fleeing the police, he escaped into the jungle and landed a job on a banana plantation. But there he contracted malaria and fell extremely ill.

One day in his feverish delirium he heard a strange voice: *"Mukasa, if you don't get saved, you will die!"* Wearily stumbling out of bed, he stepped out of his hut to see who was speaking to him. But no one was there. *"Saved? What does that mean?"* he wondered.

Three times a day over the next three days, he heard this same strange voice repeating the same mysterious message. Although he expected to die soon, surprisingly within a few days he began to recover. Months went by and his health returned to normal, but he never forgot those strange words.

One day while sitting in his hut, he overhead a customer saying to the plantation owner, "When are you going to get saved?" There was that word again—saved! Would this customer be able to explain the mystery to him?

Alex hurried out of his hut and saw the customer about to leave. He stopped him, saying, "Did I hear you say something about being saved?"

Right then and there, the man explained to Alex what it meant to be saved by Jesus Christ. As Alex heard the gospel, the Lord convicted him of its truth. He decided to accept Jesus as his Lord and Savior, and from that day onward he was a completely different man.

Alex returned to Kampala, where the police were so amazed by his change of heart that they dropped all the former charges against him! Today he leads a ministry called Back to the Bible Truth, through which 137 churches have been planted and countless believers have been trained in the Word of God. Having finally understood the mystery of salvation himself, he labors to share its truth with others who have yet to understand it.

CBCB

"... the word of God in its fullness—the mystery that has been kept hidden for ages and generations, but is now disclosed to the saints."

COLOSSIANS 1:25-26

Lord, thank you for letting me understand the mystery of the gospel that was kept hidden for ages! Please give me a chance to explain it to someone else.

ALEX MITALA, FOUNDER-DIRECTOR OF BACK TO THE BIBLE TRUTH EVANGELISTIC TEAM, UGANDA, HANDING OUT CERTIFICATES TO HIS BIBLE SCHOOL GRADUATES

74
Strength to Speak

Uganda

In the jungles of Uganda, she had encountered all kinds of dangerous wild animals. But it looked like this was going to be the most frightful experience of her life!

Catherine was going to her first ministers' conference with her new husband, Alex Mitala. He was a gifted speaker, but she had always been extremely shy. She was asked to teach a one-hour seminar for the ladies there—the very thing she feared they would ask her to do.

How could she possibly get up before all those women, many of them more spiritually mature than her? Who was she to be sharing with them? What would she talk about for a whole sixty minutes?

Her assigned topic was home management. Catherine knew that this was a great need in Uganda. Many of the ministers' wives were not raised in Christian families, so they never learned Christian principles for running a home. Like their own church members, they also faced problems in their marriages, with their children, and with their finances. Usually burdened with other people's needs, these pastors' wives had little time to address their own problems at home. Sensing these pressing concerns and clinging to the promise of Philippians 4:13, Catherine carefully prepared her message.

The day of the seminar arrived. Before she knew it, it was her turn to speak. She stepped forward and looked at the crowd. Fifty women stared back at her, hungry to hear what she had to say. In half an hour she finished saying all that was in her notes and everything that was on her heart. She still had thirty minutes left but nothing more to say!

Catherine began to panic. Her eyes scanned the audience again. She could tell from their eyes that many of these women were hurting inside. Many were tired and in need of spiritual renewal.

She invited those who wanted the Lord to do a new work in their homes to come forward. The entire group stood up and came toward the front! There at the seminar, all of them recommitted themselves to being loving wives to their husbands and godly examples to their children.

What a joy it was to see fresh peace on their faces! Since that time, the Lord has opened many doors for Catherine to speak. She regularly conducts ladies' and youth seminars throughout Uganda. And whenever the slightest fear grips her heart before speaking, the promise of Philippians 4:13 always gives her strength.

CᗺCᗺ

"I can do everything through him who gives me strength."

PHILIPPIANS 4:13

Lord, I admit that I have many weaknesses and fears. Let me always rely on You for strength to overcome them all!

75
Standing Firm

Raju finally figured out how to completely rid his village of all Christian influence. If somehow he could destroy the evangelist's hut, then surely he would have to leave!

Evangelist Prem John had come and settled in the Sikh village of Kotakpura. In spite of local opposition, he still managed to build a small hut there and began sharing the gospel. Even though some villagers had threatened him and warned him to stop preaching, Prem stood firm in his faith and refused to be cowed by their words.

But one villager, Raju, was determined to drive him out. One day after Prem had gone out, Raju went to his hut and tried to destroy it with smashing blows. But even after repeated swings, he only managed to make a small crack in one of the walls. Thoroughly frustrated, Raju stormed off.

The next morning, Raju had just left his home when he suddenly heard a strange rumbling noise behind him. He turned around and stared aghast: without any warning, his well-built house suddenly came crashing down into a heap of rubble!

The entire village was stunned. How could such a sturdy building suddenly crumble for no apparent reason? As Raju thought over this matter, he realized that it was no coincidence that he had gone to destroy Prem's house just one day before his own house collapsed.

Afraid that Prem's God might do something worse to him, Raju went straight to Prem and confessed his deed. Soon Prem was able to lead Raju and his entire family to Christ—the first Christian family in Kotakpura! From that time onward, other villagers also became receptive to the gospel, and today more than 400 attend church there.

Prem's faith, like his house, stood the storms of life because it was built upon the firm foundation of God's truth. Let us also make certain that every aspect of our lives is built upon that same foundation.

ଔଔ

"Therefore everyone who hears these words of mine and puts them into practice is like a wise man who built his house on the rock. The rain came down, the streams rose, and the winds blew and beat against that house; yet it did not fall, because it had its foundation on the rock."

MATTHEW 7:24-25

Lord, would You show me if there is any part of my life—my marriage, finances, career, education, etc.—which is not standing on a godly foundation?

76
Never Lose Heart

T he news pierced Max's heart like a sword: *"Your boy ran away."*

For years, Max Strong had been taking in abandoned and orphaned children from all over India and Nepal. More than a hundred children lived at his large Christian orphanage in northern India, receiving food, shelter, clothing, education, and the gospel.

One of his boys, George, had come there from Calcutta, where he used to run wild with a street gang. Both he and his younger brother were sent to Max's orphanage in the hope that there they would reform their ways. But the two boys were unaccustomed to structured living. They found the long list of rules burdensome and Max's preaching boring.

One day they decided to go for a swim in the local pond, which was against the rules. It proved to be a fatal mistake: George's younger brother drowned in the murky waters. Filled with guilt and hurt, George ran away. By the time Max found out about it, it was too late to track him down. After all the trouble he had taken to help these two boys, what was there to show for it? One dead body and one empty bunk. All he could do was commit the tragedy into the Lord's sovereign hands, as he had done many times before.

Many years later, Max had to travel to Calcutta for some work. On Sunday morning he decided to attend a local church for worship. When he walked inside, he was completely taken aback to see George there— well-dressed and all grown-up now. Max asked him what he was doing there. George just flashed a huge grin and replied, "Well, I'm the pastor here!"

Max listened in disbelief as George proceeded to share his testimony. After he ran away from the orphanage, he went back to Calcutta and re-joined the street gang. But as he roamed the streets, he could not forget the gospel truths he had heard during his stay at Max's place. Eventually he confessed his sins to the Lord, surrendered his life to Jesus Christ, enrolled in Bible school, got married, and began serving as a pastor! Moreover, he was also planning to take in some street boys to rehabilitate them, just as Max had done for him.

Let us never lose heart when we face disappointments in our ministry, whether to family members or to outsiders. As long as we faithfully proclaim God's Word to them, let us trust Him to bring forth fruit at the right time.

"As the rain and the snow come down from heaven, and do not return to it without watering the earth and making it bud and flourish, so that it yields seed for the sower and bread for the eater, so is my word that goes out from my mouth: it will not return to me empty, but will accomplish what I desire and achieve the purpose for which I sent it."

ISAIAH 55:10-11

Lord, please deliver me from all ministry disappointments and discouragement, and let me always be faithful in proclaiming Your Word—whether or not I see any fruit.

77
Never Too Late

MYANMAR (BURMA)

Even if he tried harder, Kya Shin could not have made more of a mess of himself. He had only succeeded at one thing: completely destroying his own life.

His problems started when he became an alcoholic. Then one day he noticed patches of swollen flesh on his body, which turned out to be leprosy. Horrified by the diagnosis, he started drinking even more furiously, hoping that alcohol would rid him of this cruel disease.

But the more Kya drank, the more unstable he became. One day during a family quarrel, he became so angry that he killed his father-in-law. He was arrested and thrown into prison, where his health continued to deteriorate as the leprosy spread further over his body. As a result, after some time the prison authorities banished him to one of Myanmar's desolate leper colonies to live out the rest of his existence.

There Kya received medical treatment, and his condition improved. Feeling better about life, Kya decided to get married again. But soon he started drinking again and also influenced his second wife to join him. After they started attending the local leper church, however, both of them decided to try to follow the pastor's advice to stop drinking.

But one day Kya caught his wife drinking secretly, and in one of his characteristic fits of rage he stabbed her with a knife. By the time his temper cooled down and he realized what he had done, it was too late. She never recovered, and with tears in his eyes he watched her die right in front of him.

Kya had finally sunk to the lowest point of his life. Alcohol, leprosy, uncontrollable anger, murder, prison, and two failed marriages—he realized that he had no one to blame but himself. Was it too late to turn his life around? He began recalling all the things the pastor had said, things that he had never before taken seriously. That day he went before the Lord with a broken heart, repented of his sins, and dedicated himself to following Jesus Christ the rest of his days.

Kya's life completely changed after his conversion. The Lord gave him a third wife, who shared his commitment to a life of godliness. As he grew in his faith, he began sensing a burden in his heart to do something for the God who had saved him and transformed his life. Eventually the Lord led Kya and his wife to go as missionaries to another Burmese leper colony, where there was no Christian witness. Today Kya serves as the pastor of a growing leper congregation there.

Let us always remember that it is never too late for even the most wretched sinner to repent.

"Christ Jesus came into the world to save sinners—of whom I am the worst. But for that reason I was shown mercy so that in me, the worst of sinners, Christ Jesus might display his unlimited patience as an example for those who would believe on him and receive eternal life."

1 TIMOTHY 1:15-16

Thank you, Lord, for saving all kinds of sinners—including me.

KYA SHIN, PASTOR OF THE SAGAING
LEPER COLONY CHURCH, MYANMAR"

78
A Praying Dad

K ateni could not believe his ears. His father—converted to Christianity? How could he have fallen so low?

Born into a Muslim family in East Java, Kateni attended an Islamic school and learned to read the Koran as a child. He worshipped at the local mosque and grew strong in his Muslim faith. Once he happened to meet some Christians, and he remembered being impressed by their good lives. But in his heart he dismissed them as misguided people, because he had heard that they believed in all kinds of foolish heresies.

One day his father told him that he had decided to become a Christian. Kateni was stunned: how could his own father reject his Islamic heritage? How could the same man who had sent him to study the Koran suddenly reject everything it said? Kateni could only conclude that his father had been terribly deceived, and he resolved never to betray Allah as his father had done.

Kateni's father began praying constantly to Jesus, loud enough for his son to hear. During his prayer time he would always pray for Kateni—that his heart might be opened to receive true peace and joy through Jesus Christ. At first, Kateni felt extremely awkward listening to his dad's prayers. But over the course of time, his heart softened and he became curious: what was there in Christianity, that even his own father could be drawn away by it?

One day he agreed to accompany his father to church. For several years he kept on attending church with his dad just to learn what

Christianity was all about. Still, his heart was not convinced. Then one day during the service, a visiting widow stood up and shared her testimony of how Jesus had filled her heart with peace. Kateni was so moved by her words that he immediately repented of his sinful pride and asked God to forgive him. From that day onward, his heart was filled with the peace and joy of Jesus Christ.

Kateni owes his salvation to a father who prayed without ceasing for him. Are you also praying without ceasing for someone else?

෴

"The prayer of a righteous man is powerful and effective."

JAMES 5:16

Lord, help me to pray faithfully for others, that they might repent and find peace with You through Jesus Christ.

79
Church Under Fire

IRAN

I t seemed like this church in Iran would not survive.

The government authorities hanged the first pastor, who left behind a blind wife and four children.

The authorities then began to harass the second pastor. They made him report to their office every week. They monitored all his activities, tapped his phone, and checked his mail. They threatened to harm his wife and children. They put pressure on his landlord to expel them from his apartment.

They told him they knew that he wouldn't mind being the next Christian martyr in Iran, so instead of killing him they had decided to continuously harass him until his life became unbearable.

One day when he returned home, he found that some of his personal things were missing. Apparently some government agents had illegally entered his home in his absence. When he went to complain to the authorities, they simply ignored his case. Instead, they ordered him to leave the city within twenty-four hours. That night he had to flee.

The authorities then began to persecute the remaining members of his church. They forced some of the families to leave for other towns and even other countries. They threatened to expel other church members' children from school. They even called in the children of the first pastor whom they had assassinated, to try to force them to convert to Islam.

For several months all church meetings were cancelled. But after some time, the believers gathered together again under the leadership of the first pastor's son. The Christians refused to let the authorities shut them down. Amidst great persecution they continue to worship the Lord there.

In spite of the martyrdom of the first pastor, the expulsion of the second, and the continued harassment of the remaining church members, this church in Iran continues to glorify the Lord and point lost souls to the cross of Calvary.

What is your commitment to the church of Jesus Christ?

C3CR

"We are hard pressed on every side, but not crushed; perplexed, but not in despair; persecuted, but not abandoned; struck down, but not destroyed."

2 CORINTHIANS 4:8-9

Lord, please uphold this church in Iran and give them strength to continue remaining faithful to You. Please also strengthen my commitment to the church.

80
A Family Feud

B iswanath was so excited about his new faith. But what would his father say?

Biswanath's father was a Hindu priest. From miles around people came to him, presenting their offerings to the Hindu gods. Only he alone was permitted to enter the temple, where he would throw flowers, sprinkle powder, or pour coconut milk at the feet of the gods. On behalf of the worshippers he would offer animal sacrifices.

Throughout his childhood, Biswanath followed all the Hindu practices and worshipped all the different gods according to the required rituals. Like his forefathers, he was a devout Hindu who never questioned his faith.

But one day he met a Christian who told him about the invisible God, Maker of heaven and earth. He was moved by the love of this God who came to earth as a man and gave His life for the sins of the world. In time, he opened his heart and received Jesus Christ as his Lord and Savior.

The joy of his salvation, however, was soon clouded by the thought of how his family would react. He knew his father was a Hindu priest, but at the same time he figured that out of love for him his father would probably accept his conversion.

But he was in for a rude surprise. As soon as his father heard that his son had become a Christian, he demanded that Biswanath renounce his new faith. When he refused, his father became furious and swung an axe at him. He managed to save himself only by ducking behind a wooden pole.

Biswanath had no choice but to flee home. The Lord kept him safe and provided for all his needs, and he grew steadily in the Lord. Eventually he enrolled in Bible college, and after graduation he decided to return home to serve as a church planter.

His father's wrath has since subsided, and Biswanath continues to pray for his salvation. The same gospel that brought peace into his own heart has also brought strife into his own home. Yet Biswanath, along with many believers around the world who go through this same struggle, knows that the Prince of Peace gives grace to bear up under even the most stressful of family situations.

CRCR

"Do you think I came to bring peace on earth? No, I tell you, but division... They will be divided, father against son and son against father..."

LUKE 12:51-53

Lord, please give me grace to be a faithful witness to those family members who are still unsaved.

81
Just an Arm's Length Away

U sha was too terrified to think clearly. Her own uncle was sending the town's leading assassin to kill her at 7:00 p.m. What should she do?

Usha never expected her own uncle to turn against her like this. A year ago while going through a family financial crisis, she had asked him for a loan so she could open a small business—a beauty parlor—to provide for her family. He agreed, but on the condition that she purchase the parlor property in his name.

Her new business soon flourished, and things were just starting to look up for her when one day her uncle quarreled so badly with her husband that he had him badly beaten up. Usha and her husband, understandably outraged, reported this incident to the police.

Angry that his own niece had turned him in, her uncle decided to teach her a lesson by putting a padlock on her parlor door. When Usha saw this, she simply cut the lock and opened her parlor for business as usual. Seeing this, her uncle got even angrier. He hired professional thugs to break into her parlor and cart everything off, down to the last hairpin. Then he threatened her: "Remember, the parlor was purchased in my name, so you are technically occupying my parlor. Unless you repay me the entire loan with interest, I'll not return any of your things!"

When Usha reported this burglary to the police, they simply ignored her and sent her away. Exasperated, she discovered that her uncle had paid them a hefty bribe to buy their cooperation. Now what? With her business completely ruined, she told her uncle, "Fine! Since you say the parlor is yours, and since you have taken away all my things, then everything for which I borrowed your money is now in your hands. So why should I bother to repay you?"

Furious that Usha seemed to be escaping from his grasp, her uncle decided to hire the town's leading underworld assassin to kill her. Usha received a call one afternoon informing that he would be coming at 7:00 p.m. to finish her off.

What should she do? She knew that calling the police would be useless. Hysterical with fear, she rushed to the home of her Christian neighbor, Indira, to seek counsel. Usha had been a Hindu all her life, but her gods were not answering her desperate prayers. Would Jesus be able to save her from this killer?

Indira confidently answered, "Usha, I know my Lord's arm is not too short to save you. Just keep crying out to Him and put your trust in Him, and He will surely deliver you. I don't know how, but He surely will!"

Up until 7:00 p.m. the two ladies kept praying to Jesus for her deliverance. At exactly 7:00 p.m. an army jeep suddenly pulled up in front of their gate: old army friends had unexpectedly dropped by unannounced. At the same time, her assassin also came; but seeing the jeep, he hastily fled—assuming that Usha had called the Indian Army for protection! In a dramatic turnaround, the assassin went to her home the next day and apologized for planning to kill her!

Usha continued to pray daily to Jesus, and within one month everything miraculously turned around for her. The local police station was censured for accepting bribes, her uncle's injustice was publicly aired in the newspaper, and she got an interest-free loan to purchase a new beauty parlor!

Seeing with her own eyes all that Jesus had done for her, she eagerly gave her heart to Him and was baptized. Today she excitedly tells others about the God who extended His arm just in time to save her.

 CR CR

"Was my arm too short to ransom you? Do I lack the strength to rescue you?"

ISAIAH 50:2

Lord, whenever I feel like my situation is hopeless, let me remember that Your arm is definitely not too short to reach out and deliver me.

82
Noah's Ark

A large boat, a worldwide flood, and three sons who repopulated the earth. Where do we find this story? In the Bible, of course. But not only in the Bible, to the surprise of some missionaries…

For centuries the Nosu tribe of southwestern China lived in mountaintop seclusion, completely cut off from the outside world. They looked down on all other ethnic groups, including the Chinese, and believed that other races existed only to serve them. A fierce, tall, warrior-like people, the Nosu used to capture the Chinese in terrifying raids and force them into slave labor.

They were animists, worshippers of many different gods and evil spirits. There was not a single Christian among them. When the missionaries arrived, they were surprised to discover that despite their pagan traditions, the Nosu still had a legend of a great flood that destroyed the earth long ago.

According to this legend, God sent a messenger to warn three sons about a coming flood. The first two sons ignored the warning, but the third son, Dum, built a boat out of wood. Twenty days later the rains came. It rained for seven days and seven nights, flooding the entire earth. After the flood, the boat landed in the snowy mountains of Tibet. When they emerged from the boat, Dum's three sons repopulated the whole earth.

The parallels between the Nosu legend and the Biblical account are fascinating. In both stories, God sent a warning of an upcoming flood. Both tell of some who ignored the warning but one man who heeded it by constructing a wooden boat. Both state that it rained day and night. Both tell of the world being destroyed by the flood, the boat coming to rest on a mountain, and the three surviving sons repopulating the earth.

Interestingly, the ancient Egyptians, Babylonians, Assyrians, Greeks, Chinese, and Native Americans all have similar flood legends. But only Genesis gives precise details such as the size of the ark, the exact height of the water above the earth, and the length of time the floodwaters remained. Comparing the Genesis account with the others, we can readily deduce that the Genesis account, with the most detailed and precise information, must be the original one. The other accounts like the Nosu one must have been passed on through word-of-mouth by the descendants of Noah who scattered throughout the earth, with many of the original details getting corrupted over time.

Let us be encouraged by one more piece of evidence for the truth of the Bible. Those who laugh off the Genesis flood story as mere fiction cannot, at the same time, provide a sound explanation for how ancient peoples around the earth all testify to a worldwide flood. Given such evidence, dare we take lightly even a single word of the Bible?

"And the words of the Lord are flawless, like silver refined in a furnace of clay, purified seven times."

PSALM 12:6

Lord, I praise You that people around the world bear witness to the truth of Your Word. Forgive me if I have taken Your Word lightly.

83
No Keeping Quiet

Sumadi Adikusumo could never have imagined that one day he would become a Christian. He grew up in a conservative Muslim family, and all of his education right up through university took place in Muslim institutions. Every Friday he spoke at the mosque, teaching fellow Muslims how to earn favor in God's sight.

His turnaround began when he attended a series of public lectures given by a leading religious scholar. The lecturer spoke about the three great monotheistic faiths: Islam, Judaism, and Christianity. Afterwards, Sumadi started to wonder: if there is only one God, then why are there three monotheistic faiths?

He felt a strong urge in his heart to learn more about Christianity, and he ended up devoting the next eight years to this pursuit. He read the Bible along with many other books, compared the Bible to the Koran, and spent long hours praying to God to show him the truth. Finally, Sumadi decided to surrender his life to Jesus Christ in 1978.

Sumadi could not keep quiet about his new faith. He wanted everyone to know the truth that had set him free from eternal judgment, sin, fear, and falsehood. He began sharing the gospel with his friends and neighbors, many of whom put their trust in Jesus. He started witnessing in his government office, even at the risk of losing his job. He witnessed to many Muslim leaders, several of whom also decided to become Christians. He even wrote and distributed booklets on how to evangelize Muslims.

Sumadi prayed day and night for his wife, who initially was so opposed to his conversion that she even tried to turn his own children against him. Finally the Lord opened her heart, and she too received the Lord. His children and his parents soon followed.

But eventually Sumadi was fired from his government job. The police arrested him, threw him into prison, and began to torture him. They said they would stop only if he agreed to deny Christ. He refused, so they threatened to kill his wife and his children. Still he did not give in, so they beat him up until he lost consciousness.

Then the authorities brought Sumadi to trial on the charge that he had tried to discredit Islam through his writings. He was sentenced to five years in prison. But not even prison could silence him: many inmates became Christians through his unstoppable witness. Since his release, he continues to testify boldly for the Lord.

Sumadi's courageous and tireless witness in the face of great persecution springs out of a burning desire to tell others about the Lord's goodness and saving love. O that we would have the same passion in our hearts!

"Then they called them in again and commanded them not to speak or teach at all in the name of Jesus. But Peter and John replied, 'Judge for yourselves whether it is right in God's sight to obey you rather than God. For we cannot help speaking about what we have seen and heard.'"

ACTS 4:18-20

Lord, please give me a passion to speak to others about what I have seen and heard concerning the transforming power of the gospel.

84
Open Doors

T hey were gone! During the night, all the people in the village somehow disappeared!

Just yesterday the three evangelists Marta, Delsi, and Samuel had arrived in this Cacao village deep in the Colombian jungle. They had come here to learn the language, so they could share the gospel with this tribe. The Cacao chief, wary of strangers but eager for gifts from the outside world, had half-heartedly agreed to let them stay among them.

Last night they had peacefully settled into their hut, looking forward to the days ahead with great anticipation. But when they got up at 5:00 a.m., all the villagers had mysteriously disappeared! Confused, the three evangelists spent the day waiting and praying. At 6:00 p.m. the villagers quietly returned, entered their huts, and went to sleep.

The next morning, the missionaries awoke to find themselves alone again. After sunset the villagers again returned, entered their huts, and went to sleep. Day after day this same strange pattern continued.

Marta, Delsi, and Samuel became extremely frustrated. They had trekked this far into the jungle to learn the language, only to find that no one was available to speak with them. So they spent their days reading the Bible and praying for an open door to reach the Cacaos.

Ten days later, the Lord finally gave them the open door they were seeking. That evening as the Cacaos were coming back from the jungle, Marta noticed that the chief's daughter was very sick. Touching the girl, she realized that the child was burning with fever. Marta made signs asking for permission to pray for her. The chief agreed, and the three evangelists prayed fervently for her healing. To the utter amazement of the chief, within two hours she had recovered and was eating normal food again!

Immediately the chief's heart opened up to the three strangers who had healed his daughter. He took special care to teach them the Cacao language, and before long they were sharing the gospel with him. What a joy it was for them to see the chief and his family receiving Christ as their Lord and Savior!

Sick people seldom refuse prayer, and we often overlook the opportunity to pray for sick friends, neighbors, and co-workers. Let us remember to take advantage of these open doors that the Lord gives us to bring Him glory.

CRCR

"Heal the sick who are there and tell them, 'The kingdom of God is near you.'"

LUKE 10:9

Lord, is there an open door before me? Give me the eyes to see it and the willingness to step through it.

85
A Greater Power

Jaibana, the village witch doctor, was the most feared man in the Cacao village. He alone knew how to appease the evil spirits, and he was given great powers by them. Everyone knew that he had brought healing to some and terrible misfortune to others.

As Jaibana watched the evangelists Marta, Delsi, and Samuel first heal the village chief's daughter and then lead her whole family to worship a new God, he felt extremely threatened. He knew he had to take drastic action against these three intruders, lest he completely lose control over the rest of the village.

One night while the three evangelists were sleeping, Jaibana entered their hut. They awoke to see him dancing, tossing powder on them and speaking pagan spells against them. They were frightened, but they knew it was not wise to try to stop him, given his high position in the village. Instead they decided to pray fervently to the Lord to deliver them from the power of Satan.

The next night he entered their hut again. Like before, he danced around them, threw powder, and cursed them. And once again they prayed to God for deliverance. This continued for five nights in a row. During the day, Jaibana sent them food to eat. The chief warned them not to eat it, because he knew it had been bewitched. But they prayed over the food and ate it anyway, and nothing happened to them.

On the morning of the sixth day, Jaibana called together all the villagers. He announced in front of them all, "These three are more powerful than I! For the last five days I have spoken every curse I know against them. I have poisoned their food and asked the spirits to destroy them. But nothing has worked! The spirits protecting them are greater than the ones I have sent against them!"

Marta asked permission to share about the Spirit protecting them. "Our God is not an evil spirit wanting to harm you, but a loving Father wanting to bless you."

As the three missionaries shared the gospel, the Lord opened the hearts of their listeners. Jaibana himself surrendered to the Lord, as did many of the other villagers. Today the Cacaos rejoice knowing that Jesus has set them free from their bondage to evil spirits.

ೞೞ

"You, dear children, are from God and have overcome them, because the one who is in you is greater than the one who is in the world."

1 JOHN 4:4

Lord, I rejoice that You are greater than any other power in the world! Help me to fully grasp what this truth means in my life.

86
A Deeper Peace

I t took only one rumor to shatter the peace. The stars were quietly shining down upon Shantinagar, which means "Town of Peace." One of the few Christian villages in Pakistan, her people know a faith nurtured deep through many trials. But on the night of February 5, 1997, their treasured peace erupted, and they found that faith put to the supreme test.

That day a local Muslim tailor claimed to have found pages torn out of the Koran with blasphemous statements written on them. Because the pages were found in a small mosque near Shantinagar, it was automatically assumed that someone from the local Christian community had done this. There was not a shred of evidence, but no one seemed to care.

The rumor spread like wildfire throughout the district. Motorists drove around everywhere proclaiming the blasphemous incident. Announcements were made from mosques urging Muslims to unite and march to Shantinagar to avenge the horrible desecration.

The Christian villagers discovered what was happening and immediately went to the police to request protection. But their plea fell on deaf ears, as the police had already sided with the rumor-mongers.

In a matter of hours, an angry mob swarmed the streets of Shantinagar. They first ransacked the church, the pastor's home, and the school. Then they sprinkled gasoline on the carpets to burn down these buildings. They went from house to house and shop to shop, looting and torching everything in their path. They beat up the men, abused the women, and drove away their cattle. They snapped the town's water supply and electricity lines.

The police did nothing to stop the violence. Instead, they joined the rioters in beating up the Christian villagers. Eventually, the armed mob swelled to 30,000, and not until the army intervened the next morning did the mob finally disperse and the destruction come to an end. But by then it was too late. In that short period of time, 1,500 houses, shops, and buildings along with thirteen churches had burned to the ground.

The villagers of Shantinagar are slowly rebuilding their lives. They will never forget the violence of that February night. Yet in the midst of their sufferings, they also know that the only true peace available to them is the deeper peace offered by Jesus Christ.

Do you know that peace?

ം8ിം

"I have told you these things, so that in me you may have peace. In this world you will have trouble. But take heart! I have overcome the world."

JOHN 16:33

Lord, in the midst of my trials and hardships, let me know the over-coming peace that You alone can give.

87
Alive and Well

Without any warning, they suddenly burst through the door of the small village church just as the service was beginning. They called for Shantilal, the pastor. Caught off guard, he stepped outside—only to receive a hard blow that knocked him down to the ground. Before he knew what was happening, iron rods rained down upon him. The assailants then dragged both Shantilal and another evangelist, Rajendra, back into the church. Right there in front of the other church members, both of them were brutally beaten until they lost consciousness.

The thugs now directed their violence towards the other believers. The room echoed with screams of terror as they began attacking everyone in sight. Not even the women and children were spared. Blocking the only door of escape, the attackers continued their assault until every last believer was down on the ground and the floor completely stained with blood. Then they stormed off.

When he regained consciousness, Rajendra's chest ached with intense pain from the blows he had suffered. But despite his injuries, he was more concerned about the future of this little church. Rajendra knew firsthand what it was like to undergo persecution, for he was the first in his village to become a Christian. After his conversion, his parents along with the local authorities threw him out of the village. But the Lord took care of him, leading him to another state and providing him with a job there. Eventually he went to Bible college.

For his three-month ministry assignment, he had come here to Udaipur to help the local pastor, Shantilal. Everything was going smoothly until this terrifying incident took place. After this, Rajendra wondered if the young church would still survive.

The following weekend, Shantilal and Rajendra could hardly contain their joy as the recovering believers all gathered at the church for the service. Moreover, that very day ten people committed themselves to follow the Lord and were baptized! The two Christian workers praised the Lord for turning Satan's attack into an opportunity for harvest.

Persecution has never stunted the growth of the church, and this was no exception. The church in Udaipur is alive and well!

CʒCℜ

"Dear friends, do not be surprised at the painful trial you are suffering, as though something strange were happening to you. But rejoice that you participate in the sufferings of Christ."

1 PETER 4:12-13

Lord, when it is our turn to suffer for You, please remind us to endure it cheerfully, for You have suffered so much for us.

88
The Testimony of Moajem Khan

BANGLADESH

"For twenty long years I searched for the truth in the Holy Koran but was never satisfied. One day in my search, I read something in the Koran that I had never noticed before. The verse said that Isa (Jesus) is the spirit of Allah and the revelation of Allah. I wondered about this and thought that perhaps I had stumbled upon something significant in my search for the truth.

"One day in the marketplace I met a man, Abdul, who had left our traditional ways to follow Isa. I shared with him what I had read, and he became very excited. He explained to me that if I wanted to know more about Isa, then I should read the Inzil Sarif (New Testament).

"As I began to read this new book, I learned that Isa was not just a man like the other prophets but rather God Himself. I learned that Isa became a man in order to save sinners like me. I was so happy to hear this that I decided to accept Him as my Savior and obey Him in baptism. In my joy I shared everything I learned with my family. Now my wife and three children are also believers in Isa.

"The other villagers hate us. They always talk bad about us and criticize us. But praise God—now a few others have also become believers in Isa!

"I am a primary school teacher, and I also work in the fields. But still I always try to make time to tell others about my faith. Presently almost 100 people around me are open to hearing about Isa. Every week people come to my house to learn more from the Inzil Sarif.

"I wanted to learn more, so I went for short-term Bible training. It was not easy for me to go, leaving behind my family and my work. Moreover, I am almost 60 years old and my eyesight is not very good. But God helped me through the classes so I could grow in my faith.

"Please pray for me and my family. Sometimes we feel lonely because we are cut off from our relatives and neighbors. From time to time they come and threaten us. Please pray that we may stand strong in the Lord. Pray that the Lord will help us get a place of worship. And pray that I will be able to help others follow Isa."

CʒCʒ

"If you suffer as a Christian, do not be ashamed, but praise God that you bear that name."

1 PETER 4:16

Lord, please give grace to Moajem and others like him who are insulted for their faith. Let them not be put to shame, but rather let them see Your hand of deliverance.

89
From Darkness to Light

After Kiatisak began studying the Bible, his soul became troubled with many disturbing questions. Foremost among them was, *Will Buddha punish me for being unfaithful if I become interested in Jesus Christ?*

Kiatisak grew up in a Buddhist family in Thailand. As the eldest son, he had to set a good example for his younger siblings. For eighteen years he faithfully studied the Buddha's teachings and honored him through daily offerings of incense, food, and flowers.

He could still remember the day he was ordained into the Buddhist priesthood. Older monks shaved his head and eyebrows. Then he went off to the temple in an elaborate procession witnessed by all his relatives and close friends. After parading three times around the temple, he went inside to meet the head monks who were waiting for him. He recited the Ten Precepts for Buddhist novices in the ancient Pali language, in which he vowed to refrain from such worldly acts as stealing, drinking alcohol, dancing, singing, lying on a bed or mattress, watching entertainment, and eating between noon and sunrise.

After he left the priesthood, he continued his education in Bangkok. There he heard of a place where he could learn English for free, as long as he agreed to attend a Bible study afterwards. Eager to learn English to improve his career opportunities, he began attending both the English classes and the mandatory Bible studies.

For six months Kiatisak was not at all interested in the Bible. But then the Word of God began to stir his heart. As his interest grew, his soul became filled with many questions. *Why did his parents worship him when he was a Buddhist priest? Did they realize that the saffron robes he used to wear on the outside never changed his heart on the inside? Would Buddha punish him for his interest in Jesus?*

In time, Kiatisak became convinced that he was a sinner in need of salvation. On December 6, 1968, he prayed to receive Jesus Christ as his Savior. For the first time in his life, his soul was filled with true peace and joy.

Amidst much persecution from family and friends, Kiatisak grew in the Lord and eventually obeyed God's call to the ministry. Today he is one of the key leaders of the Christian community in Thailand. More than thirty years later, he continues to boldly proclaim the power of God that brought an ex-Buddhist priest out of darkness into His wonderful light.

CSCR

"But you are a chosen people… a people belonging to God, that you may declare the praises of him who called you out of darkness into his wonderful light."

1 PETER 2:9

Lord, may all who feel empty in their souls come to know the One who alone can fill their hearts with peace and joy.

90
A Surprise Confession

His roommates could not believe what they were hearing from Abdul's own lips in the middle of the night. Had he gone completely mad?

Abdul grew up in a Muslim home where all the members of his family spoke to each other in Arabic, the holy language of Islam. While he was still a young man, his father sent him to study at a special school to become an eloquent preacher of the Koran.

On the way to his new school, Abdul received a little Arabic booklet from a fellow traveler. He read through it several times before realizing that it was a piece of Christian literature—the New Testament book of Philippians. He was about to throw it away, when he suddenly felt an invisible hand restraining him. Puzzled, he decided to tuck the booklet into his handbag. But the words of Philippians 2:5-8 kept on ringing on his head.

Once he reached his new Muslim training academy, Abdul forgot all about this incident and immersed himself in his studies. Three and a half years later, he suddenly woke up one night with the words of Philippians 2:5-8 ringing again in his head. The impression was so strong that he had to search his handbag for the Christian booklet given to him years back. After locating it, he read it over and over again until dawn.

For the next seven nights in a row, he woke up at midnight with the same words ringing in his head. And every night Abdul would whisper a prayer: *"Lord, is it true that Jesus Christ is in very nature God? Please reveal the truth to me!"* On the seventh night he re-read the book of Philippians, and the words of 2:10-11 burned in his heart: *"Every knee should bow... and every tongue confess that Jesus Christ is Lord."* No longer able to contain his inner struggle, he finally shouted aloud, "Jesus Christ is Lord!"

Abdul spoke so loudly that all of his friends in the dormitory also woke up. Startled, they asked him what had happened. He answered, "I confess that Jesus Christ is Lord!" His friends told him that he was out of his mind and was demon-possessed.

The next morning, the schoolmaster summoned Abdul and ordered him to retract what he had said the previous night or else face expulsion. Without any hesitation Abdul answered, "I confess that Jesus Christ is Lord, to the glory of God the Father! I will not retract my confession, because God has been trying to reveal this to me ever since I left home three and a half years ago!"

Abdul was expelled from the school. The Lord led him to a Christian who clearly explained the gospel to him, and he received Jesus Christ as his Savior. Although his family completely disowned him, he continued to remain faithful to the Lord. Eventually he enrolled in a Christian training center, and presently he serves as an evangelist to his own Muslim people.

Though it cost him dearly, Abdul chose to confess—this side of heaven—that Jesus Christ is Lord. Woe to those who wait until the Last Judgment to acknowledge this! Have you made your confession already?

"At the name of Jesus every knee should bow... and every tongue confess that Jesus Christ is Lord, to the glory of God the Father."

PHILIPPIANS 2:10-11

Lord, may my confession of faith in You remain steadfast until the end.

91
More Than Skin Deep

The sight of his arms was hideous. The smell, even worse. Fernando had covered them with a towel to ward off the flies. What would the doctor say?

Fernando Cagulong had traveled fifteen miles into town with his wife to get emergency medical treatment for his rotting arms. They had gone from doctor to doctor, all of whom had prescribed different medicines for him. One week later, they had exhausted all of their funds, but still his arms were no better.

Then they heard about a Christian medical outreach in town. As a last resort they went there for help.

"We've been to several doctors, but nothing has worked," wept Fernando's wife. "We have no more money left. Please, can you do something for my husband?"

Even the doctor squirmed as she lifted up the towel and saw Fernando's arms—two masses of swollen raw flesh. She hated to tell patients bad news, but she knew it was not wise to give them false hope either.

"I'll give you an antibiotic for the infection and an antifungal ointment," the doctor said, "but I must be honest with you. If you had gotten treatment earlier, everything would have been fine. Now it's rather late. However, we are Christians, and we believe in a living God who can heal all kinds of diseases. Would you let us pray for you?"

Without any hesitation Fernando and his wife agreed. The doctor gathered the other medical outreach workers and together they all prayed for Fernando.

Three days later, Fernando and his wife returned to meet the visiting pastor who had organized the outreach. At first the pastor did not recognize him, as his whole appearance had completely changed.

"Look at me, sir! Do you recognize me?" Fernando asked with a wide grin.

The pastor studied him closely. Was it really Fernando? He was completely healed! There was not a trace of fungus and not a single scar on either his arms, face, or the rest of his body, which was formerly covered with rashes. "The Lord has answered our prayers and healed you!" exclaimed the pastor.

Right then and there, Fernando received Jesus Christ into his heart. With great joy he returned to his village as a living testimony to the Lord's power. His family became the first Christians in his village, and they helped start a church there which now has 70 members.

03 03

"But as for me, I will always have hope; I will praise you more and more. My mouth will tell of your righteousness, of your salvation all day long."

PSALM 71:14-15

Lord, let me also be a living testimony to Your power so that I can lead others to Your feet.

92
The Cost of Commitment

A Christian man was called in by the Muslim authorities in the Iranian city of Shiraz. They ordered him to give up his Christian faith, or else he would have to give up his job.

He replied, "It is better to be poor than to stop being a Christian." He was fired from his job.

After some time they summoned him again and ordered him to give up his faith, or else they would expel his son from school.

He answered, "It is better for my son to be illiterate than for me to stop following Jesus Christ." His son was suspended from school for seventeen days.

After some time they summoned him a third time and ordered him to give up his faith, or else they would expel him from the city.

He replied, "If you force me to go, I will have to leave. But I will never turn away from Jesus Christ."

He and his family were forced to leave the city. He asked the other church members to pray for him: *"Pray that I can carry my cross all the way to Calvary and not put it down in the middle of the road."*

The cost of commitment is high, but it is trivial compared to the rewards waiting on the other side for those who have faithfully walked in the footsteps of their suffering Savior. Are you among that crowd?

"Be faithful, even to the point of death, and I will give you the crown of life."

REVELATION 2:10

Lord, may You find me faithful in counting the cost of commitment to You.

93
What Has Your God Done?

His Muslim parents did not know what to do. Nothing, it seemed, could remove the doubts that plagued their son day and night.

Since childhood, Idir had followed all the Muslim rituals. Even so, his soul still burned with doubts. He kept wondering, *Where is the true God, and how can I know him?* But his family just told him to follow their traditions and their prophets, like all good Muslims. It did not take long for Idir to realize that those whom he considered as his spiritual leaders were lost themselves, because they spoke with so little conviction.

His parents thought that getting married would take their son's mind off these religious questions, so they arranged a wife for him. But still his doubts persisted. Unable to handle this nagging stress, he decided to go to France, leaving behind his family, his country, and his doubts. There, far away from home, he indulged himself in all kinds of worldly pleasures. Yet emptiness and discontentment also followed him there.

One day Idir met some Christians. They asked him if he knew Jesus. "I know he was the son of Mary and Joseph," he replied.

"But would you like to know how He can live in your heart and change your life?"

"I am a Muslim," he answered.

"No problem. Let us share with you what Jesus has done for us, and then you tell us what Mohammed has done for you."

As they shared how Christ had delivered them from their sins and filled their lives with new meaning, Idir could hardly believe their words. They spoke of Jesus as a close friend.

"Now you please tell us what Mohammed has done for you."

Idir thought and thought, but nothing came to mind. "I am somewhat embarrassed, but I can't think of a single thing," he finally admitted.

"You've been a Muslim your whole life, and you can't think of even one thing that Mohammed has done for you? Then why not come along with us to our meeting and learn more about what Jesus can do for you?"

Hesitantly, Idir agreed. As he heard the speaker, he realized that all the answers he had been seeking lay in the message of the gospel. Before long he surrendered his heart to Jesus Christ. Idir later returned to Algeria and led his wife and mother to the Lord. Today he runs a radio ministry that broadcasts to his own people the same eternal truths that changed his life.

Idir was led to the Lord by friends who shared what the Lord had done for them. Have you told someone lately what the Lord has done for you?

"For you are great and do marvelous deeds; you alone are God."

PSALM 86:10

Lord, would You give me a chance to tell someone about the great things You have done for me?

94
Sorcerer to Saint

BENIN (WEST AFRICA)

K oudedo was the chief sorcerer in the village of Awonsedja. The villagers lived in such fear of him that they used to regularly give him money and other gifts just to remain on his good side, lest he turn against them and pronounce terrible curses upon their heads.

But after some time, the villagers could no longer tolerate his threats. They decided that the only way to get out from under his terrifying power was to kill him.

One day they set Koudedo's house on fire. They were stunned, however, to see him emerging from the flames—alive! He boasted all the more that no force or power could conquer him, and the villagers became even more afraid of him. Only one man—Valentine the evangelist—was not bothered by his boastful claims to power.

Koudedo became increasingly annoyed with Valentine, because he alone refused to cower before him. Didn't this man recognize what a mighty sorcerer he was? Determined to put him in his place, Koudedo challenged Valentine to a fight. "I'm coming to your house," he warned, "and then we'll see who is afraid of whom!"

Valentine went home to pray and waited for Koudedo's visit. Three days later, Koudedo sent three shrieking birds in the middle of the night to Valentine's house. The evangelist immediately woke up and realized that his rival was using one of his sorcery techniques on him. He confessed aloud to the birds, "Jesus is Lord!" and they stopped shrieking and flew away.

The next day Valentine met Koudedo on the street. At the sight of the evangelist, Koudedo immediately turned and bolted in the opposite direction. Valentine called out to him, but Koudedo kept running away because he realized that Valentine was powerful enough to defy his curses.

After returning home, Koudedo fell seriously ill. Several days later, Valentine was led by the Lord to go and pray for him. At last Koudedo recovered, and then he admitted that he also wanted to follow the greatest power—Valentine's God. Thus the mighty sorcerer of Awonsedja gave his heart to Jesus Christ.

Let us always remember that we Christians should never be afraid, because no power that we will ever encounter—whether human or supernatural—will ever surpass the power of our God.

ങ്ക്ര

"Say to God, 'How awesome are your deeds! So great is your power that your enemies cringe before you.'"

PSALM 66:3

Lord, I praise You for being more powerful than any other person or spirit in the world. Let me never be afraid of anyone or anything.

95

Flung from the Family

INDIA

Furious over his son's conversion, Pranab's father tried to kill him and his mother nearly poisoned him. What should he do now?

Pranab Mukherjee was born into a high-caste Brahmin Hindu family in eastern India. Like the rest of his family, he was an idol worshipper. His parents were planning on him becoming a Hindu priest one day.

When he was 17, two evangelists came to visit his town. After he learned they were Christians, he threatened them: "If you don't leave this place immediately, I'll kill you!" Despite his harsh words, the evangelists still spoke warmly to him and gave him a New Testament.

Pranab could not put out of his mind the great love he felt from these two men whom he had tried to harm. After some time, he decided to read the book they had given him. Surprisingly, his heart was touched from the very first verse. He wanted to learn more, but he could not fully understand what he was reading.

To get answers, he visited a man who had once been a Hindu Brahmin like himself but who had later decided to become a Christian. That man clearly answered all of his questions and explained to him the gospel in detail. Pranab's heart was deeply moved and eventually he decided to receive Jesus Christ as his Lord and Savior. Then his soul was flooded with a deep peace, and he felt as though a great weight had been lifted from his heart.

Pranab did not tell his parents about his conversion, because he knew what their reaction would be. But one day they caught him reading the Bible, and they understood that he had become a Christian. His father was furious. "We are high-caste Brahmins," he shouted, "and you have accepted a low-caste religion! You cannot remain in our family any longer!"

Picking up a large hammer, his father swung hard at Pranab's head. His aunt rushed over to protect him, and the hammer crushed her upraised hand instead. Pranab immediately told his father he would leave home. His mother asked him to first eat before leaving. While eating, he noticed that the milk she had served him tasted funny. He poured it out, and several cats came to lap it up. Within a few minutes they were dead. He then understood that his mother had poisoned his milk.

Pranab knew he had to leave immediately. But where should he go? He first went to the home of the man who had led him to the Lord. Later he watched in awe as God provided for his needs time and time again. Eventually he went for Bible training, and afterwards the Lord called him to start a church-planting ministry in eastern India.

Though he had been flung from his own family, Pranab found the Lord to be a never-failing refuge and deliverer. Have you also made Him your refuge, too?

"The Lord is my rock, my fortress, and my deliverer; my God is my rock, in whom I take refuge."

PSALM 18:2

Lord, let me always look to You and You alone to be my refuge and my deliverer.

PRANAB MUKHERJEE, FOUNDER-DIRECTOR OF
CARE AND SHARE MISSION, INDIA,
WITH HIS WIFE PRATIBHA AND DAUGHTER ASHIMA

96
Crushed But Not Broken

INDIA

O ut of nowhere the vehicle suddenly appeared, slamming straight into the evangelist on the motor scooter.

Torn away by the sudden impact, Kingsley flew several feet in the air until he struck the road hard, fracturing his right arm and leg. In the next instant the vehicle emptied, and he found himself surrounded by a group of Hindu fanatics cursing and beating him mercilessly. Again and again pain surged through his battered body.

They dragged him all the way to their compound. All the while Kingsley continued to writhe in pain. Bystanders had gathered to watch, but no one dared to interfere.

Finally an elderly man in the crowd stepped forward. "Stop it," he pleaded, "or you will kill him!"

The assailants clubbed Kingsley one more time. "If you don't stop your preaching, next time we'll kill you!" With that, they let him go.

When Kingsley arrived home, his wife and children burst into tears upon seeing him. Immediately they took him to the hospital. Later four members of the same fanatical Hindu group came to his wife and threatened her: "If you and your husband continue to engage in conversion activities, we will surely kill you all!"

It took three months for Kingsley to recover. During this time, he and his wife prayed about their future. Despite the death threats, both of them sensed that the Lord still wanted them to stay where they were and continue to preach the gospel. Knowing that the police and the government had turned a blind eye to this brutal incident, they realized that they could only depend upon the Lord for protection.

To this day, Kingsley and his wife continue to trust in the Lord amidst numerous trials and difficulties. And because they have chosen to depend completely upon the One who promised to remain with them always, He has upheld their cause and enabled them to continue forging ahead for His kingdom.

Have you completely made the Lord your only place of trust?

C３CR

"We do not want you to be uninformed, brothers, about the hardships we suffered... We were under great pressure, far beyond our ability to endure, so that we despaired even of life... But this happened that we might not rely on ourselves but on God, who raises the dead."

2 CORINTHIANS 1:8-9

Lord, in my troubles and trials, teach me to fully put my trust in You.

97

The Power of the Word

O f course, it was an unusual gift for a Hindu priest. But all the same, Resham still accepted it, not knowing that it would completely change his life.

Born into a high-caste Brahmin Hindu family in Nepal, Resham Poudel became a Hindu priest. His days were spent performing Hindu rites and offering sacrifices of cow milk, rice, flowers, and animals to the different gods.

He never questioned his beliefs until the day he received a copy of the New Testament as a gift and began to read it. As he read about the life and character of Jesus, he realized that none of the Hindu gods could compare with Him.

He read that Jesus "came to seek and to save what was lost." This was in complete contrast to what the Hindu scriptures said about one of the main Hindu gods: "I came to save the righteous and kill and destroy the sinner." He also read that heaven was a free gift to all who believed, in contrast to the Hindu teaching that each person had to perform many good deeds and go through many reincarnations before reaching heaven.

The more Resham read the Word of God, the more convinced he became of its truth. In time, he decided to become a Christian. When his family learned of his conversion, they were furious. How could a Brahmin priest join the cow-eating religion? They threw him out of the house.

But the Lord was with Resham and directed his steps. As he continued to read the Bible, the Lord put a strong burden in his heart for the thousands of Hindu villages in his country that had never heard the name of Jesus.

For the past four decades, Resham has endured every manner of hardship for the Lord, including hunger, imprisonment, and landslides. He has been arrested 22 times for preaching and thrown into prison three times. Once while he was preaching in prison, the guards threatened him if he did not stop. Resham answered, "It was because of my preaching that I was thrown into prison in the first place. So where else will you send me if I continue preaching now?" Through his prison ministry many fellow inmates have become Christians, and some of these are serving as pastors in Nepal today.

The Word of God transformed a proud Hindu priest into an unstoppable evangelist. What effect has the Word of God had in your life?

♋♋

"'Is not my word like fire,' declares the Lord, 'and like a hammer that breaks a rock in pieces?'"

JEREMIAH 23:29

Lord, may the Word of God radically transform my life, too.

98
Drafted into the Lord's Army

THAILAND

W hat is a Christian supposed to do when he runs into seventeen homeless families and there isn't a homeless shelter to refer them to? This was the dilemma facing Somboone, a simple but God-fearing man who desired to do the Lord's will.

Somboone had not always been so simple and God-fearing. Born in southern China, he and his friends were drafted by the Chinese army to fight against Burma. After he saw his friends dying one after another in battle, he decided to run away from the army to save his own life.

Somboone took refuge in a small Burmese village, where he heard the gospel for the first time and received Jesus Christ as his Savior. As he grew in his faith, he became convicted that the Lord was calling him to be a preacher. The ex-Communist soldier was now drafted into the Lord's army.

Two decades later, Somboone was traveling through the mountains along the Thai-Burmese border when he came across seventeen homeless families from a tribe known as the Palaung. Although he did not know their language, he came to learn of their terrible plight through an interpreter.

These Palaung families had been living peacefully in Burma until the day government soldiers suddenly invaded their village without warning. They beat up the men, assaulted the women, and torched their homes. From that day onward, these Palaung families had been wandering as refugees, desperately looking for a place to re-settle. But nobody wanted these foul-smelling, illiterate Buddhist peasants near them. By the time they had trekked their way across the border into Thailand, they were sick, exhausted, and despairing of life.

Upon hearing their story, Somboone was moved with compassion. He invited all seventeen families to come and stay with him in his own village, where he gave them huts to live in! After settling them, he began to tend to their illnesses. He prayed for one very sick man, who was soon miraculously healed.

Amazed that Somboone's prayer was answered, the Palaungs wanted to know more about the God to whom he prayed. But how could he tell them about the Lord, when he could not even speak a word of their language? He decided to show them a Thai film about Jesus and requested those children who had learned Thai in the refugee camps to translate it for the adults. After watching the film, all seventeen families decided to become Christians!

Somboone not only serves as the pastor of this impoverished Palaung community but also as their provider. He supplies them with food and also helps them find employment. Besides shouldering all this responsibility, he continues to travel as an itinerant evangelist, preaching the gospel in other villages where the name of Jesus has never been heard.

O, for a whole army of dedicated soldiers like Somboone!

"Endure hardship with us like a good soldier of Christ Jesus. No one serving as a soldier gets involved in civilian affairs—he wants to please his commanding officer."

2 TIMOHY 2:3-4

Lord, would you please give me the discipline and single-mindedness to be a dedicated soldier of Jesus Christ?

SOMBOONE AMORNSANTIKHIRI,
EVANGELIST TO THE PALAUNG TRIBE, THAILAND

99
No Laughing Matter

When someone told him that Jesus was the only way to heaven, Amir just laughed. How could anyone, especially a mullah (Muslim priest) like himself, believe in such a foolish notion?

But after hearing this statement, Amir was suddenly seized with a strange curiosity to learn more about Jesus. He secretly visited a local church and picked up a copy of the Gospel of John. He read it cover to cover 25 times. Although the message about Jesus seemed like sheer nonsense to him, there was still a deep urge within to learn more.

One verse particularly grabbed his attention: *"I am the way and the truth and the life. No one comes to the Father except through me"* (John 14:6). It kept on ringing in his head, even though he tried his best to forget about it. He prayed several times to cast it out of his mind. But the more he prayed, the more it consumed his thoughts.

After a few days, Amir developed a severe pain in his head. Afraid that God was punishing him because he had read a Christian book, he locked himself in the mullah training school for seven days to seek pardon from Allah. At the end of the seventh day, Amir again heard the same voice in his head: *"I am the way and the truth and the life. No one comes to the Father except through me."* Exasperated, he got up and left the building. Immediately he felt a strange peace settling in his heart.

Amir then decided to see a doctor about his head pain. After examining him, the doctor remarked that he had all the symptoms of a brain tumor. Not knowing what to do, Amir went out for a walk around town the next day. As he was passing by the church, he noticed that a meeting was going on inside. He wondered: *did God bring me this way for a reason?* Ignoring the prohibition against mullahs entering churches, Amir walked right in and sat down in the front.

During the entire service, Amir listened intently to every single word. Incredibly, the sermon that evening was based on John 14:6—*"I am the way and the truth and the life..."* Everything the preacher said made complete sense to him, and by the end of the sermon all his doubts had disappeared. When the preacher gave the altar call, Amir jumped up from his seat and went forward to receive Jesus as His Lord and Savior.

After his conversion, his headaches never returned. He revisited the doctor, who concluded that his brain had mysteriously returned to normal. Amir soon enrolled in a class for lay ministers, to grow in his new faith. Unable to contain his excitement, he began telling everyone he met about his conversion experience. Most of them just laughed at him and some even beat him up, but still he refused to keep quiet about the Lord.

Truly, Jesus is the way, the truth, and the life—for people of all nations and from all religious backgrounds!

"I am the way and the truth and the life. No one comes to the Father except through me."

JOHN 14:6

Lord, I praise You for showing me that You are the only way, the only source of absolute truth, and the only path to true life.

100
Kagi and the Great Physician

T he doctor did a double take when she saw Kagi, the Muslim village chief, in her town clinic. Was this a divine appointment?

Dr. Nora ran a private clinic in the town of Norala. She also had a strong burden to use her medical skills to serve the Lord. So together with several of her colleagues, she began visiting the surrounding Muslim villages to provide basic medical treatment to the poor.

One Muslim village they visited was led by a chief named Kagi. Although he knew that Nora and her colleagues were Christians, he still allowed them to visit his village because he needed their medical services. He always watched them curiously from a distance whenever they visited.

Villagers rarely came into town, so Nora was taken aback one day when she suddenly saw Kagi standing there in her town clinic. Her initial surprise immediately faded, however, when she saw his sick daughter at his side. The girl's neck was dreadfully swollen, and Kagi pleaded with Nora to do something to help her.

After examining the girl, Nora realized that she was suffering from diphtheria in its final stages. "I'm sorry," she told Kagi, "but there is nothing I can do for her at this point."

Tears welled up in Kagi's eyes. For once, the village chief had lost his normal composure. Desperate to help, Nora decided to try the only possible remedy left. Bowing her head, she prayed in the name of Jesus for the girl's healing.

To Kagi's astonishment, the swelling in his daughter's neck began to subside. Before long, her health was completely restored! Kagi was beside himself with joy. Overwhelmed with gratitude, he decided to give his heart to the God who had saved his daughter's life.

Kagi returned home and excitedly shared with the other villagers what the Lord had done for him. As a result, his entire village turned to the Lord. Today he and his fellow villagers gather in their own church to praise the God who continues to heal the sick and give life to the dead.

෫෮෮

"And the prayer offered in faith will make the sick person well; the Lord will raise him up."

JAMES 5:15

Thank you, Lord, for Your healing power over our bodies and souls.

Advancing Native Missions:

A CHALLENGE TO RESPOND

After reading these testimonies of what the Lord is doing in the uttermost ends of the earth, you may be wondering, "Can I be a part of what is happening in the lives of these native missionaries?"

Yes! **Advancing Native Missions (ANM)** is a non-denominational U.S.-based missions organization that serves as a bridge linking individuals and churches in the West with native missionaries in other parts of the world. Through ANM, many Western Christians have been able to partner effectively with native missionaries to reach unreached and unevangelized peoples with the gospel.

WHY NATIVE MISSIONS?

Today, native missionaries are the fastest, most efficient, and most economical means of taking the gospel to unreached and unevangelized people groups. Without significant language or cultural barriers, without the need to obtain government entry visas, and living at a similar socio-economic level as those they are reaching, native missionaries are bringing tens of thousands of souls to the Lord's feet daily. Traditional foreign missionaries, though faithful and hardworking, cannot complete the task of world evangelization alone. What we cannot do alone, we can do together!

How Does ANM Identify These Native Missions?

ANM's international staff travels around the world visiting native missionaries to understand and evaluate their mission activities. We partner with native mission groups which subscribe to an evangelical statement of faith, which are open and transparent in their finances, and which work among unreached or unevangelized people groups. We also consider spirituality, effectiveness, growth, and leadership quality. ANM particularly recommends native mission groups which are fruitful in winning souls, planting churches, training missionaries, and caring for needy children.

How Can You Be Involved in Serving Native Missionaries?

1. Pray for native missions. Use the stories in this book to pray for native missionaries. Or contact ANM and request us to send you regular mission newsletters on any of the ministries mentioned in this book or in any part of the world.

2. Sponsor one or more native missionaries. Through ANM's Missionary Sponsorship program, your financial gifts will go directly to the missionary's group. We will send you a picture of your missionary as well as regular newsletters from the mission under which he or she serves.

3. Sponsor a child. Through our Child Sponsorship program, you can help save a child twice: once from poverty and neglect, and second from a Christ-less eternity. We will send you a picture of your child as well as periodic updates.

4. Provide funds for needed equipment. Through our Mission Projects department, you can help purchase Bibles, books, bicycles, scooters, and other vital equipment needed by native missionaries.

5. Go personally to visit and encourage native missionaries. Through ANM's Operation Barnabas International department, you can be part of a team that goes on-site to encourage, train, and learn from native missionaries.

6. Invite ANM to conduct a missions conference at your church. Upon request, we will send our Building the Kingdom Together (BKT) team to your church to conduct a missions conference, free of cost. Visiting native mission leaders will join us whenever possible to inspire your church to be actively involved in missions both at home and abroad.

What is ANM's Financial Policy?

ANM purposes to be open and transparent before God and man in the stewardship of the gifts entrusted to us by the Lord's people. We deduct 7.5% of all incoming gifts for administrative purposes. A financial statement is available upon request. ANM is a member of the Evangelical Council for Financial Accountability.

HOW TO CONTACT ANM

For more information about ANM or to request more copies of this book, please visit our website at www.adnamis.org or contact us at:

Advancing Native Missions
P.O. Box 5303
Charlottesville, VA 22905

Phone: 540.456.7111

Fax: 540.456.7222

Email: anm@adnamis.org